Cracking the Carbon Code

Cracking the Carbon Code

The Key to Sustainable Profits in the New Economy

Terry Tamminen

First published in 2011 by
PALGRAVE MACMILLAN®
in the United States—a division of St. Martin's Press LLC,
175 Fifth Avenue, New York, NY 10010.

Where this book is distributed in the UK, Europe and the rest of the
world, this is by Palgrave Macmillan, a division of Macmillan Publishers
Limited, registered in England, company number 785998, of Houndmills,
Basingstoke, Hampshire RG21 6XS.

Palgrave Macmillan is the global academic imprint of the above companies
and has companies and representatives throughout the world.

Palgrave® and Macmillan® are registered trademarks in the United States,
the United Kingdom, Europe and other countries.

ISBN: 978–0–230–10950–6

Library of Congress Cataloging-in-Publication Data

Tamminen, Terry.
    Cracking the carbon code : the key to sustainable profits in the new
economy / by Terry Tamminen.
        p. cm.
    ISBN 978–0–230–10950–6
        1. Emissions trading. 2. Carbon offsetting. I. Title.

HC79.P55T36 2010
363.738′74—dc22   2010025760

A catalogue record of the book is available from the British Library.

Design by Newgen Imaging Systems (P) Ltd., Chennai, India.

First edition: January 2011

10 9 8 7 6 5 4 3 2 1

Printed in the United States of America.

For Constantino Cruz, Diana Wrightson, Drew Bohan, Michael Northrop, Craig Cogut, and the many others who have shown us that climate change creates both challenges and opportunities—but that the path ahead is up to us.

CONTENTS

LIST OF ILLUSTRATIONS

Figures

Tables

FOREWORD

In my early days of bodybuilding, I remember working so hard to lift 50 pounds, then 100, then 300. After years of exercise and competition, I could lift 480 pounds, but wanted to beat the Austrian record of 500 pounds. Everyone at the gym said it was impossible. Even I had my doubts. But I knew that to win the ultimate bodybuilding championship, Mr. Universe, my muscles had to be strong enough to bench press that 500-pound barbell.

I tried week after week, five times, eight times, ten times, but could never lift that much weight. It was just 20 pounds more than I had already lifted, and no matter how many times I failed, I kept working to add muscle and become strong enough to beat the record. Any reasonable person would have settled for 480 pounds, but I was determined to prove the skeptics wrong and push myself to a new level. Finally, after what seemed like endless training, workouts, and setbacks, I thrust that barbell high over my chest—with 501 pounds of weight on it, a new record!

The lesson I learned from that experience was that no matter how hard it appears, every worthwhile goal can be accomplished. You have to set the goal and then organize every step along the way until it builds up to victory. You must evaluate the obstacles so you can overcome them—are they mental barriers or physical ones? Are they perception or reality? What will it take to do something no one has done before?

The same has been true for me as Governor of California, tackling the twin goals of building a strong economy and protecting the environment. I introduced the Million Solar Roofs Initiative to power the state with clean energy from the sun, for example, but each year the measure was defeated by the state legislature.

I kept working on it with Democrats and Republicans, with labor leaders and home builders, with environmental groups and chambers of commerce. On the third try we got it done. Today, we are more than halfway toward our goal of a million rooftops in California generating both clean energy and sustainable, high-paying jobs.

In recent years, the world's economy and its glaciers have experienced a simultaneous meltdown for many of the same reasons. The *solutions* to these problems are also intertwined and present us with a fantastic opportunity for a century of unparalleled growth and prosperity for everyone. But we must first set new goals for the way we think about energy and work toward them step by step.

Energy is a fundamental building block of any economy, not to mention any business or family budget. When gasoline prices double in a matter of weeks or when electricity grids can't keep up with demand, businesses close and workers are laid off. This breaks budgets around the world and such volatility makes it impossible to plan for other needs.

I remember the 1973 Arab oil embargo. It was just a few years after I arrived in America, and the lines went around the block to fill up our cars. What if we had a choice back then, to use a different fuel or to fill up with fuels that didn't depend on a single source? What if we had that choice now, when many families must choose between putting $50 into their gas tanks instead of food on their tables? Reducing our dependence on carbon-based fuels can help us get out of the current financial mess; and greater energy diversity means long-term energy security.

But can clean, renewable fuels be enough to power our economy in the twenty-first century? Consider this: enough sunlight falls on the earth every hour to power all of humanity's energy needs for a year. And did you know that there's enough hydrogen in the water discharged by sewage treatment plants to power all of our cars, trucks, trains, and airplanes? Add to these the potential of biomass, geothermal, tidal power, wind, and other renewable sources and it's clear that there are enough clean energy resources, but we must deploy the technology to use them, especially technologies that make more of what we already have. We've done it in California. For example, we have set energy efficiency standards for appliances and buildings that make us 40 percent more energy efficient than average Americans. I recently toured a company in San Francisco, Solazyme, that makes fuel for the Navy from algae. Our Hydrogen Highway Network is demonstrating that cars powered by the most abundant, clean resource in the universe can create even more new businesses, and freedom from unreliable, polluting fossil fuels.

In *Cracking the Carbon Code*, my friend Terry Tamminen provides us with a compelling playbook of how to restore our economic vitality and preserve our environment for generations to come. Businesses can save money and grow markets by reducing their carbon footprints. Governments can create public-private partnerships to invest in low carbon technologies, making schools, public facilities, and fleets into leaders of green building and transportation designs. People around the world can compete with each other to see which company, state, or nation can slash its carbon the most, with a goal of reducing greenhouse gases at least 80 percent by 2050. And we shouldn't wait to see who goes first, but race to the head of the pack.

Of course there are many complex solutions to our economic and climate change challenges, but in the end, igniting this fundamental shift will depend on bold action by government, business, and each one of us. This won't be a spectator sport. There are no innocent bystanders now that we know what's at stake.

So let's get on with it! Together we can lift the heavy weight of the economic and climate change challenges facing us today, and make everyone a champion for generations to come.

—GOVERNOR ARNOLD SCHWARZENEGGER

ACKNOWLEDGMENTS

The benefits of cracking the Carbon Code would not have materialized in the United States without the bold leadership of Governor Arnold Schwarzenegger. Because of his political risk-taking in California, the rest of the country is unlocking the secrets of the Carbon Code and the federal government has now begun to follow. This, in turn, gives us all hope for a global agreement that will result in a sustainable environment and economy in the twenty-first century. We owe him a great debt of gratitude.

Of course, as the old saying goes, success has many parents. My team at Seventh Generation Advisors has contributed to this book and helped California push forward on the low-carbon path and shown other governments and businesses around the world to learn from its example. Thanks to Kristina Haddad, Sasha Abelson, Andria Mack, and Jenna Cittadino. Thanks also to my partner and friend Bonnie Reiss, who served with me in the Schwarzenegger administration and made the climate policy work possible. She and her colleague Nick Kislinger remain instrumental in implementing that vision in the business world today.

Just as Al Gore first spoke to Congress about climate change in the early 1980s, there was one shrewd strategist who not only saw that states would be the living laboratories for a low-carbon economy before the rest of us did, but also put the strength of a major foundation behind numerous NGOs to develop and implement the policy details. Thanks to Michael Northrop of the Rockefeller Brothers Fund (ironically, a foundation with an endowment built on oil wealth) for being that visionary a decade ago and introducing me to the idea that we need not wait for national governments to get things done.

I also owe a great deal to Eric Heitz, Marcus Schneider, Jane Bloch, and the team at the Energy Foundation. In 2003, tasked by Governor Schwarzenegger to recommend carbon reductions for the state and the means to achieve them, I realized that my staff at the California EPA had no time and limited expertise for such a monumental project. I turned to the Energy Foundation for help and they pulled together the scientists, policy experts, and economists that helped us draft the Climate Action Plan, which ultimately became the state's Global Warming Solutions Act of 2006 (AB32). Their support since then has resulted in numerous countries and companies discovering the benefits of energy efficiency, renewable energy, and a host of other measures that make cutting carbon both possible and cost effective.

With the creation of AB32, it took a dedicated team that works both inside and outside of government to make a low-carbon future possible. Thanks to the entire CalEPA and CARB teams, but especially to Linda Adams, Alan Lloyd, Mary Nichols, Drew Bohan, Patty Zwarts, Anne Baker, Margret Kim, Eileen Tutt, Maureen Gorsen, Clay Russell, and the unflappable Will Fox.

Of course if policies are enacted but no companies respond with products and services that replace our fossil-fueled habits (and if consumers don't embrace those transformational companies), it's like clapping with one hand. Thanks also goes to the smart investors, such as Craig Cogut and the team at Pegasus Capital Advisors, for proving time and again that a sustainable environment is the fundamental building block of the most profitable, sustainable economies and for their contributions to this book.

Telling a story and providing advice verbally is one thing, but putting it on paper is quite another. Thanks to Cynthia Cannell and Bruce Tracy for helping me wrangle complicated material into a usable format in this book, and to my editor at Palgrave, Laurie Harting, for getting it onto bookshelves.

Finally, I often joke that I could end global warming single-handedly if I stopped flying around the world. While an exaggeration, it highlights the weeks spent away from home and the fact that I could not have undertaken the work described in this book without the love, support, and advice of my wonderful wife Leslie Tamminen and our son Jake Rubin.

On behalf of generations yet to come, who will live with our success or failure in making the profound transition to a truly sustainable world, my gratitude to everyone who is helping world governments and businesses to crack the Carbon Code—and secure the path to sustainable prosperity in the new economy of the twenty-first century.

INTRODUCTION

What Is the Carbon Code?

Carbon emissions. Carbon tax. Cap-and-trade. "New" economy.
California Governor Arnold Schwarzenegger and Chinese Minister Xie Zhenhua.
AB32. AAUs/CERs. CDM & JI. CFCs. CO2. COP15. EU ETS. GHGs. ICAP. IPCC. ISO14064. RPS. UNFCCC. WCI/RGGI/MWGGGA.
The Japanese town of Kyoto.

This dizzyingly varied jumble of people, places, concepts, and acronyms are all oddly shaped pieces of a mosaic that, taken together, equal a new owner's manual for the economy of the twenty-first century. Along with hundreds of new laws, incentives, politics, inventions, Nobel Prize winners, science debates, and disappearing natural resources, it all adds up to something called the *Carbon Code.*

Simply stated, the six "greenhouse" gases emitted from decaying materials and the combustion of fossil fuels—called "carbon" for short—are a surprisingly effective means to measure efficiency and waste. The more carbon emitted from a power plant, for example, the less efficient is that combination of fuel and generator. Those inefficiencies can be measured and mitigated, saving money and limited natural resources in the process. The Carbon Code sets out the practical steps for making almost any business more efficient and shows how to use this unique yardstick to understand the costs and benefits of each marginal improvement.

Of course not all companies are direct emitters of carbon, but most rely on those that are, such as power plants, transportation, waste disposal, and buildings (yes, even an office tower is a major source of carbon emissions). Businesses, investors, shareholders, governments, and consumers are being inundated with complex and conflicting data points about climate change and the efforts to address it. The book in your hands puts all of this dynamic information into a comprehensible order and context. It provides a road map through the maze to help you understand what parts of this new economic paradigm will fundamentally change the way we do business, the way we choose our investments, and even the way we make choices about allocating the planet's remaining natural resources.

Anyone working at an oil refinery, for example, already knows they must measure and report carbon emissions to USEPA. So do managers of the other 10,000 installations across the United States and 15,000 across Europe in industries with similarly large and obvious carbon footprints. But what about manufacturers, or their suppliers, of the hundred thousand products on Walmart shelves? What about businesses that don't realize their operations may hide liabilities so vast that companies "too big to fail" will soon be dropping in value, or even from the marketplace altogether? Everyone with money to make—or lose—needs to understand how to crack the Carbon Code and how to make profitable use of this information.

This book will not only reveal the secrets of the Carbon Code, but it will give you the amazing background of how it was developed and introduce you to the fascinating people and places to watch for future changes and opportunities. Those who crack the Carbon Code will be able to spot the companies and technologies that are to the new low-carbon economy what Microsoft and Apple were to the information technology revolution of the 1980s.

Liabilities avoided. Fortunes made. The wiring instructions of the future made simple. This is what *Cracking the Carbon Code: The Key to Sustainable Profits in the New Economy* is all about.

CHAPTER 1

The Bodybuilder, the Brit, and the Oilman:
A Brief History of the Carbon Code

Never was so much owed by so many to so few.
Winston Churchill, August 20, 1940

It was a warm and muggy Southern California day in July 2006, but no hint of perspiration dared to appear on the bronzed face of Governor Arnold Schwarzenegger. He was speaking with Lord John Browne, then chairman of oil giant BP (known then as British Petroleum), and me at a port facility in Long Beach. We were waiting for the arrival of British Prime Minister Tony Blair.

The topic of this summit was putting a price on greenhouse gas pollution—"carbon"—and its genesis was straightforward. A year earlier, The Governator had addressed a crowd in the San Francisco City Hall on the United Nations' World Environment Day, declaring "the science is in; the debate is over; the time for action is now," and set California's goals for reducing carbon—down to 1990 levels by 2020 and 80 percent below that by 2050. He signed an

Executive Order that day establishing a path to achieve those goals, but any truly meaningful regulation of carbon would depend on putting all of this into law, because industries such as oil, cement, agriculture, and the catch-all California Chamber of Commerce quickly lined up to criticize the governor's action as a job-killer and business-buster.

Despite the misgivings of some, by early 2006 state agencies and a multitude of stakeholders had developed a credible plan that would achieve the carbon reductions and pay for much of it with energy efficiency measures, renewable energy generation like solar and wind power, and the production of alternative fuels like hydrogen, bio-diesel, and batteries—all things that would make California more competitive and create new industries in the Golden State. To convert the plan into law, the governor worked with legislators to introduce Assembly Bill 32 (or simply "AB32"), The Global Warming Solutions Act of 2006.

Locked in a tough re-election campaign and with his own Republican Party firmly opposing AB32, Schwarzenegger began campaigning to get the bill passed. In June, Schwarzenegger and I had flown to Sedona, Arizona to attend the Western Governors' Association annual meeting. We had successfully convinced the other governors at the meeting—conservative Republicans and liberal Democrats alike—to sign an agreement to tackle climate change on a regional basis. We needed this kind of broad support to make the case back home for AB32, but the meeting high-lighted another challenge: addressing global issues on a less than global scale.

As we prepared for the formal session where the regional deal would be adopted by the nineteen governors, we compared notes on carbon policy with two other progressive governors—Janet Napolitano of Arizona and Christine Gregoire of Washington. Janet was smart and articulate, qualities that would later bring her to the attention of President Obama and put her at the head of the federal Homeland Security Agency. Christine was a bold risk-taker. She had just won her first term in office, after a recount, by a mere 200 votes (taking Seattle with a 150,000 vote majority, but losing the rest of the state by an equally large margin), highlighting the sharp partisan divisions in her own state. Tackling climate change would be popular in the big city, but feared and opposed everywhere else.

Of all the opposition arguments, the one that seemed to be the hardest for all three governors to overcome was the idea that if only a few states imposed limits or costs on carbon, it would drive businesses to other parts of the country and ultimately wouldn't do much to tame greenhouse gas emissions. We concluded that someone would have to recruit more governors to adopt similar policies, a de facto national climate action plan.

Like Schwarzenegger, I had come to Sacramento to take a turn at public service, not to become a career civil servant. I had served as secretary of the California Environmental Protection Agency and later as Schwarzenegger's cabinet secretary, managing policy for all of state government, but had planned to stay no more than one term. In the absence of federal policy, the three governors knew they needed a "climate ambassador" to help other states figure out how to develop their own climate action plans and to get them working together on regional policies around sharing renewable energy production and creating a market for carbon emission reductions. It seemed like a natural fit for a policy wonk, who came from a nonprofit think tank, to go back to that world and to begin to connect the dots with other states. I was deputized on the spot, but needed a carbon-plated calling card to showcase as a template for other governors. AB32 would have to become law in California for any of this to succeed elsewhere.

"How Much Did You Pay Him to Say That?"

The 2006 Western governors' meeting culminated with a unanimous agreement to collaborate on climate change policy. Even with that endorsement and a growing number of progressive California business interests voicing support, Schwarzenegger still needed one more push to get AB32 across the election-year political finish line, so we organized a CEO forum and persuaded BP to host it at their port facility in Long Beach, California on

July 31, 2006. CEOs of global businesses that had prospered under European carbon regulation were asked to share their experience with CEOs of U.S. companies that could influence state lawmakers to support a carbon reduction law. We secured one more key component of this campaign—the keynote speaker at the event would be British Prime Minister Tony Blair.

Years before the massive 2010 oil spill in the Gulf of Mexico tarnished its reputation, BP was the perfect host for a business event focused on the environment—an oil company that conducted business on both sides of the Atlantic and declared its famous initials stood for "Beyond Petroleum." Lord John Browne could testify to the benefits of a lower-carbon future and show off a new oil tanker that ran on cleaner fuels and operated at greater efficiencies and therefore lower cost. A sparkling white tent had been set up to hold the forum on the docks adjacent to the tanker, green plastic grass covering the oil-stained pavement inside.

Blair's motorcade came speeding into the compound in a cloud of dust and tires grinding on gravel. Schwarzenegger strode purposefully out into the blazing afternoon sun and extended a hand to Blair as he emerged from the car. As the two leaders strolled toward the tent, chatting intently about how to convince the assembled business leaders that a low-carbon economy was in the best interests of their shareholders, the governor gestured for me to join them.

"Terry, I want you to hear this," he said, prompting Blair to repeat what he had been saying.

"As host of the G8 last year, you may recall I took on climate change as one of our key topics," Blair said as if conducting a graduate seminar on public policy. "We invited the five biggest developing countries [China, India, Brazil, South Africa, and Mexico] to join us on this topic, because without their cooperation, we will never solve the climate crisis. They made it very clear that their countries would not reduce carbon emissions unless the United States does so. I was just telling the governor that in the absence of U.S. federal policy, that makes what California is doing *so* important to the rest of the world. But I also mentioned that it wouldn't be enough to get these developing countries to move if *only* California takes these actions. We need California to convince other states to do the same, sort of a de facto national climate plan."

"So how much did you pay him to say that?" Schwarzenegger asked me with a big grin. We explained to the puzzled Blair that just a few weeks ago in Arizona, we had decided to take our show on the road and help other states adopt California-style climate and renewable energy policies.

"Oh, that's brilliant," Blair said with a mixture of relief and glee. "You *must* do so. You *must* succeed."

Once inside the tent, Blair and Schwarzenegger got the progressive CEOs to tell their stories and talk about what had helped them reduce carbon and save money in the process. Google founder Sergy Brin, dressed in a T-shirt and cargo pants with a solar-powered backpack recharging his cellphone, sat next to Sir Richard Branson of Virgin Group, both advocating new ways of doing business in sharp contrast to the old. They were flanked by CEOs Chad Holliday of DuPont, Mike Morris of American Electric Power, Kevin Davis of Man Financial, Jeff Swartz of Timberland, and James Murdoch of British Sky Broadcasting, among others. Together, the companies represented at the table that day earned half a trillion dollars a year and employed more than 300,000 workers.

Perhaps the most persuasive speaker was Jacques Dubois, CEO of insurance giant Swiss Re America, who warned of massive liability for insurance companies if governments failed to address climate change impacts. Around the large square table, one by one, they debated and moved the conversation from "if" to "how" and "how soon."

With support from business, the California global warming law passed, was quickly signed by the governor, and the world's seventh largest economy officially joined the global fight to slash the world's addiction to carbon. Four months later, after campaigning across the state in a green bus adorned with scenes of Yosemite and blue skies, Arnold Schwarzenegger was re-elected governor of California by twenty points over his challenger. Polls confirmed that his environmental accomplishments, particularly his leadership on climate change solutions, were the major factor in his victory.

The DNA of the Carbon Code

Globally, there are many building blocks of the Carbon Code, but within the United States, California's AB32 is the fundamental DNA upon which every other carbon regulation is built. As such, it is also the key to understanding where to look first for trends in regulation, incentives, and examples of how to unlock hidden carbon value—or liability—in almost any company.

California's actions stand on the shoulders of European policies, which were born of the United Nations' "Earth Summit" in 1992 (see Appendix B for more detail), when 189 countries—including the United States—signed the United Nations Framework Convention on Climate Change (UNFCCC), a global, though voluntary, commitment to slash carbon emissions. In Kyoto, Japan in 1997, the signatories made the deal more specific and enforceable. In the so-called "Kyoto Protocol," the United States and 38 other industrialized nations agreed to cut carbon about five percent below 1990 levels by 2012. Under the theory that developed countries had created the climate change problem (and become wealthy doing so), the developing nations had no specific obligations initially, but agreed to make some additional voluntary efforts to stem the growth of carbon too.

As a result of these initial efforts, primarily by Europe and California, to address both the challenges and the opportunities of dealing with climate change, other U.S. governors began to understand the power of the Carbon Code to change both political and economic fundamentals. With the AB32 template in my pocket, I started my ambassadorial duties and was stunned by how many states wanted to get on the bandwagon. I racked up frequent flyer miles from Annapolis to Carson City, from Madison to Olympia, from Albany to Des Moines (Appendix D describes actions taken by states to cut carbon, largely based on California's example). In early 2007 the concept spread beyond U.S. borders when Schwarzenegger received a call from

Gordon Campbell, premier of the Canadian province of British Columbia.

Premier Campbell and his policy team were eager to hear about our newly-minted carbon law, but also wanted to understand the Carbon Code behind AB32 and the programs that would achieve its goals. We had set up a program to deliver 20 percent of California's electricity from renewable energy by 2010 and one-third by 2020. We set aggressive building and appliance efficiency standards and created incentives for people to rapidly adopt them in practice. We set tailpipe emissions standards for cars and established a market for carbon so future reductions could be met by trading for the lowest-cost "credits." In all, more than 200 programs in our climate action plan—the "wiring instructions" of the Carbon Code—were set to achieve California's world-leading carbon-reduction targets.

Campbell had been a very "green" mayor of Vancouver before becoming premier of British Columbia. He ordered his team to take the best of California's Carbon Code and combine it with land use and transportation policies that he had perfected in Vancouver, creating a climate action plan unique to his province. A month after our meetings, Campbell announced his plans to cut carbon in his annual "speech from the throne," the Canadian version of a State of the State speech.

"The science is clear," Campbell had declared in his speech, channeling the one Schwarzenegger had delivered on World Environment Day some 18 months earlier. "It leaves no room for procrastination. Global warming is real."

"The B.C. government is trying to out-green California with a sweeping strategy unveiled Tuesday to fight global warming by cutting back on greenhouse gas emissions from everything from cars and industry to the daily energy consumption of ordinary people," reported the Vancouver *Sun* after the speech. "Following the script of California Governor Arnold Schwarzenegger, who rode the green wave to a landslide election in 2006, Premier Gordon Campbell is promising to head a climate action team that will demand two proposed coal-fired plants pump 100 percent of their emissions into the ground. It will adopt California's automobile emission standards starting in 2009 and encourage citizens to conserve through personal energy audits."

The premier pledged to cut BC's carbon at least 33 percent by 2020, in part by working with California, Oregon, Alaska and Washington "to develop a sensible, efficient system for registering, trading and purchasing carbon offsets and carbon credits."

Campbell and Schwarzenegger knew that Europe was considering the creation of a marketplace for emissions reductions to meet its Kyoto Protocol commitments, trading so-called "carbon credits," and that these kinds of market-based mechanisms were essential elements of the Carbon Code that could help businesses to reduce their carbon footprints at the lowest possible cost. At that 2006 Western Governors' Association meeting in Arizona, we had discussed using a similar tool among our states because of its appeal to businesses—one way to ensure acceptance of carbon-reducing policies and targets.

Adding a Canadian province would make the market and the benefits bigger, but there was still one big catch. We needed to get enough U.S. states into such a scheme to make it workable—and enough states to convince the U.S. federal government to adopt it as a national and international solution to the climate change challenge.

With British Columbia now the "California of Canada," we turned our attention to a conspicuous blank patch on the carbon-cutting map of North America. The southern states, their politicians now among the most vocal skeptics of climate change science and policy, were completely absent from the growing carbon policy coalition. Could the United States ever accomplish any meaningful national program with such a large and influential part of its geography moving in the opposite direction? Could a new president and congress be elected in 2008 that took climate change seriously without southern state support?

As it turned out, the keys to both were in the hands of a charismatic former quarterback from the Wake Forest Demon Deacons, who had just won the most important game of his political career and was now needed to lead a team into the environmental "Super Bowl"—although he didn't know it just yet.

From White Spaces to the White House

Although the two politicians may never compete at weightlifting, Florida Governor Charlie Crist could certainly give California's movie star governor a run for his money in any warm-smile-and-firm-handshake competition. A football quarterback in college, he converted his leading man good looks, sharp intellect, and earnest conversational style into a winning streak of state political posts that culminated in the governor's mansion. As attorney general, he challenged traditional thinking, often taking positions at odds with his own political party and base of support. Hoping that he might break with southerners who opposed carbon-reducing policies, I asked Schwarzenegger for an introduction.

Meeting in his office in Tallahassee within a month of his 2007 inauguration, I sat with the Florida governor and his policy advisors and laid out a series of maps of the U.S. states—those colored in green had climate action plans; those colored in blue had renewable energy mandates; states in yellow had adopted California's greenhouse gas limits on cars; states in red were copying California's AB32 and considering binding greenhouse gas reductions—just as if they were separate countries under the United Nation's Kyoto Protocol.

On map after map, one thing became clear. The entire southeastern part of the United States was white. Florida, as the economic powerhouse of the region, could be a major leader on climate and clean energy policy in the fastest-growing part of the country. In doing so, Crist could fill in the last major blanks—literally and figuratively—on the U.S. map and, therefore, on the path to getting a new global climate agreement.

"Without the Southeast, Governor," I concluded, "we'll never be able to convince Washington to adopt a credible answer to climate change. And Prime Minister Blair told us that without the United States, China, India, and other developing nations won't step up either, which means we won't have a global agreement to solve this challenge any time soon. In short, Governor—and not to put too much burden on your shoulders—you and Florida are at the tipping point. The world's solution to climate change is in your hands."

Crist studied each map as if it were a holy relic and was clearly memorizing what he saw. He put down the papers and looked me straight in the eye.

"We have to act," he said simply.

Four months later at a climate summit in Miami, adapting the Carbon Code to Florida law and politics, Governor Crist signed executive orders that spelled out his climate action plan, including renewable energy, energy efficiency, greenhouse gas reduction targets, biofuels, and a host of other carbon-busting measures, all based on California's climate change programs. Florida, and therefore the Southeast, was now in the game and another white space on the map could be colored green.

As with Schwarzenegger's introduction of the initiative in California, however, not everyone was impressed. At the summit's press conference, the first question to the governor challenged the assumptions he made prior to adopting these policies.

"Many scientists still disagree that global warming is happening," a reporter blurted out like an angry radio-talk-show host. "Who did you rely on that informed you otherwise?"

"Terry Tamminen," Crist said with a grin, pointing at me, standing off to his right. I was now a marked man. My quiet diplomacy was no longer a secret. That may have helped however, because more calls came in from U.S. governors, Canadian and Australian premiers, the European Union, China, and a candidate running for president of the United States.

Carbon Is Red, Blue, and Green

As 2007 became the year we colored the map one state at a time, journalists began to note how odd it was that Schwarzenegger and Crist, joined by Governors Rell of Connecticut and Pawlenty of Minnesota, were all Republicans. Why was the leadership for solving the climate crisis coming from the party that was thought by many to be hostile to this type of regulation?

In retrospect, it's not odd at all. Republicans are often also noted for their focus on economic issues. Those governors had been among the first to crack the Carbon Code because they understood that shifting from unreliable, polluting fossil fuels to inexhaustible, clean, renewable fuels made good business sense; that efficiency saves money; that things like green buildings and hydrogen-powered cars were going to make companies very wealthy in the near future—and that such companies could generate jobs and tax revenues in their states.

These economically driven leaders knew the benefits of harnessing markets to solve problems, especially when new low-carbon technologies could create carbon "offsets" with an estimated market potential of a trillion dollars annually by 2015. Numbers like that evoke memories of Silicon Valley and how it powered the California economy. Smart leaders wanted a piece of that action this time, before it all went to another state or another nation.

On Earth Day in April of 2008, *Newsweek* showed Governor Schwarzenegger on its cover spinning the globe like a basketball. *Vanity Fair* named both of us as environmental heroes. The world beat a path to California to figure out how he had been so persuasive when the Bush administration and much of Congress still dismissed climate change as a naturally occurring weather pattern. At Yale University that day, Schwarzenegger challenged the world to get rid of its guilt and get on with the urgent work at hand, telling them the technology needed to solve climate change would make us happy, healthy, and very wealthy.

Other governors and state legislators, eager for any way to get the kind of positive press that California's governor was reaping, took notice. By July of 2008, thirty states had adopted some part of California's Carbon Code blueprint and were developing their own climate action plans, renewable energy mandates, and energy efficiency incentives (see Appendix D for an up-to-date list of these states and their progress).

The growing number of state and provincial allies were also building a North American carbon market that would rival the one just underway in Europe. Ten northeastern states were designing a system that would cap emissions from power plants; led by California, thirteen western states began working on a market covering all sectors of the economy; nine midwestern states agreed to follow; and all three regional efforts were joined by a dozen Mexican states and Canadian provinces, forming a formidable emerging carbon marketplace across North America (see Appendix C for the current list of participants and the progress thus far to create this massive carbon market).

There was now bipartisan support for cutting carbon, covering more than half the U.S. economy—and therefore the potential votes in Congress—but still no champion who could get the federal government to take climate change as seriously as it was being addressed in state capitals. In the midst of one of the most bitterly partisan presidential elections in U.S. history, I was given the chance to explain the Carbon Code to a senator from Illinois and help him become that champion.

July 10, 2008, was a hot, humid day in Chicago. Presidential candidate Barack Obama had just finished a grueling day of campaigning, made worse by a week of delays caused in part by a broken airplane. By 9:00 p.m., though, he strode into a conference room at his campaign headquarters as though he were moving from one lecture hall at Harvard to the next, ready and eager for his next class debate.

For the next two hours, Obama moderated a briefing/debate between me, Daniel Yergin (Pulitzer Prize–winning author of *The Prize*), Peter Darbee (chairman and CEO, Pacific Gas & Electric), Jim Rogers (chairman and CEO, Duke Energy), John Rowe (chairman and CEO, Exelon), James Mulva (chairman and CEO, Conoco-Phillips), Peter Robertson (vice chairman, Chevron), John Rowe (chairman and CEO, Exelon Corporation), Kevin Knobloch (president of the Union of Concerned Scientists), John Holdren (the Harvard University professor who went on to become President Obama's science advisor), and a few other energy experts and staffers. We all agreed to the Chatham House Rule, meaning we could talk about the meeting but not attribute specific quotes to any of the participants. By the end of the session, however, we all agreed on the fundamental policy initiatives that we were recommending to the man who became the 44th president a few months later.

Those policies included an urgent and immediate emphasis on energy efficiency, because technologies that save energy can be paid for with savings on electric bills, and because most other initiatives to address climate change take far longer to show results. Even the oil company representatives agreed to promote fuel-efficient cars and driving techniques, saying that the four-dollar-per-gallon gasoline price that was prevalent at the time wasn't good for their business—it led to Congressional finger pointing and other consequences that outweighed the short-term profits. They agreed that a stable gasoline price, albeit probably higher than most consumers would like, was in their best interest over the long run, and that this was only achievable if people conserved and supplies evened out around the world. We talked about the state of climate science, technology solutions, and the states that had already blazed the trail. The next president, we all agreed, could get ahead of a parade that was already moving down Main Street and start leading it up Pennsylvania Avenue.

In that session, we made the case for an economic policy that rewards efficiency instead of waste and is based on endless clean energy resources instead of scarce, unreliable, and volatile ones. We explained to the candidate that the world, including the majority of U.S. states, had already begun to put a price on carbon, something that would fundamentally alter the course of economics in a world that was increasingly one large marketplace. We showed him that environmentalists, energy experts, oil companies, and utilities could agree on much more than one would imagine and that despite some differences, these trends would soon result in the first steps toward the decarbonization of America—a day that would likely arrive during the tenure of the next president.

Obama skillfully moderated the debate, testing each of us on the pros and cons of our positions and assertions. We watched him synthesize the information and feed it back to the group as potential policies for Congress or the next president, in each case asking us to describe how our constituents would benefit or be impacted. Congress and the American people were debating these same issues at the time, in part because oil had topped $120/ barrel and gasoline prices were soaring. More domestic oil drilling? Some kind of renewable energy stimulus package? A massive energy efficiency campaign? In each case we tried to evaluate which measures could simultaneously protect the economy, the environment, and our national security.

When the meeting ended, I had the distinct feeling that it had been helpful to Obama, but had left him frustrated by the same uncertainty about a path forward that was then paralyzing Washington DC. As many politicians called for more domestic oil drilling and questioned the wisdom of adding a new cost to the economy during tough times (and in an election year at that), it was not hard to understand Obama's hesitation. As he thanked each of us individually for participating in the discussion, I decided to use our moment alone to provide him with one more tool that would help him crack the Carbon Code and address many of his concerns about navigating the tricky political waters of Congress—if he was elected in a few months' time.

The federal Clean Air Act gives a president the authority to regulate pollutants known to harm the public. A recent Supreme Court decision had ruled that greenhouse gases were indeed pollutants under the Act. As such, an Obama USEPA could review the facts and issue an "endangerment finding"—the prelude to a purely executive-branch regulatory approach to reducing greenhouse gases—but one that could be implemented using carbon markets and the other successful initiatives already being undertaken by more than half the states.

Senator Obama asked several questions that tested my meager legal knowledge, but smiled with the satisfaction of a complete answer that had eluded him during the meeting. He now knew how to unlock the Carbon Code if he became the next president and if Congress failed to act. As he had done during the meeting, he quickly absorbed the new knowledge and challenged me to address an obstacle that the United States alone could not overcome.

"So whether Congress or the next president moves the United States, what happens if China doesn't get moving just as quickly?" Obama asked, mostly thinking out loud. "I don't suppose you can persuade China too, eh?" He chuckled as we shook hands, but as I walked back out into the rain, his question underscored the urgency of attending a secret meeting that was scheduled to take place on the outskirts of Beijing just a few weeks later.

Carbon Zen: Breaking the U.S.-China Deadlock

When details for the U.S.-China carbon policy meeting arrived, I was told we would be taken for three days to the "Commune by the Great Wall." My wife started to hyperventilate and wanted to shackle me to the great wall in our Santa Monica backyard, but I assured her that I'd be fine, because all the Chinese government wanted was insider information about American intentions regarding carbon policy. Of course I had no evidence to back up that assertion, but boarded the flight anyway with Obama's challenge fresh in my mind and knowing that Beijing might hold the key to carbon policy progress in Washington DC.

Approaching Beijing is like landing in the fog of San Francisco, except the thick gray haze that obscured the Chinese countryside was not water vapor. Even as the plane taxied, the smell of burning sausage filled the cabin, thanks to Beijing's legendary smog. With the Olympic games starting in five weeks, I wondered how athletes would fare in these conditions that were quite literally breathtaking.

Legions of crisply uniformed, multi-lingual greeters stood by to assist each traveler through the gleaming glass and steel city that is the Beijing airport, each rehearsing for the millions of visitors expected in two weeks for the 2008 Olympic Games. A driver awaited me and my wife's concerns rattled around the back of my head as kilometers ticked off, a landscape of factories giving way to apartment blocks, which gave way to villages and finally farmlands. My cell phone had lost any connection to the outside world half an hour earlier and the road signs, which near the airport were in both English and Chinese, now displayed only Chinese characters.

The car turned up a hilly road, only partially paved, past a guard with a drab olive-green uniform and a 1930s-era carbine, and soon we arrived at a modern bamboo wood and glass reception area with a peaceful fountain surrounded by lush landscaping. In the original invitation, my host had omitted a key word from the location's name—it was the "Commune by the Great Wall *Kempinski,*" a former government outpost that had been taken over by the international hotel chain and converted into a conference center. A hundred acres of steep hills and thick forest were punctuated with apartments and meeting spaces that had been re-designed by award-wining architects to blend into the scenery and utilize only the most sustainable building materials and modern conveniences, including wireless Internet.

A pleasant young man in a bellman's uniform several sizes larger than his slender frame lugged my bag up the hill to my accommodations. He used what English he could muster to ask where I was from and, when I said Los Angeles, he grinned broadly and proclaimed "Kobe Bryant Number One!"

Over dinner that night and meetings the next two days, I joined several other experts from the United States in describing likely carbon regulation under the next president, either McCain or Obama, and the path to a new global climate deal from our various viewpoints. The Chinese delegation was headed by Xie Zhenhua, who had served as the first director of China's EPA (officially the Chairman of the Chinese Commission for Certification of Produce Conformity and Environmental Standards) and was now responsible for designing and implementing China's energy and climate policies as Vice Minister of the National Development and Reform Commission.

Xie is a quiet, bespectacled civil servant, quick to laugh at himself and equally quick to recite carefully rehearsed government policy positions. Behind the demeanor of a Communist Chinese bureaucrat straight from Central Casting, Xie hid a secret that ultimately led me to believe he was courageous enough to break this pointless deadlock between our two countries.

While teaching engineering in the 1970s in Beijing at Tsinghua University, often called "China's MIT," Xie joined the Communist Party and began volunteering for various community organizing duties. He also devoted time to studying environmental law and green building techniques, working his way from academia to politics. Ultimately he was tapped to head China's new Environmental Protection Agency. In late 2005, a chemical spill in China's Songhua River threatened water supplies for millions of people in China and Russia, causing the usual spate of international recriminations. Rather than allow colleagues in the agency to lose both "face" and their livelihoods, Xie resigned his post, apparently headed to ignominious obscurity.

Because such a high-ranking official had accepted the blame, no one else was seriously punished for the incident. A deputy general manager of PetroChina was given a "demerit" on his personal record and the provincial EPA director received a "serious demerit" on his record. In fact, the explosion and spill had occurred because one technician had made a mistake in operating a critical piece of refinery machinery, not because Xie or his agency had failed in their duties.

Quietly hailed as a self-sacrificing hero by anyone who knew the facts about the chemical spill, Xie may have been sidelined, but he was certainly not forgotten. As Chinese officials grappled with growing both the economy and the necessary energy supply, while fending off mounting pollution problems and challenges about climate change, they considered creating a new Energy Agency to take responsibility for the solutions to these vexing conundrums. During his absence from government, the engineer and scholar in Xie led him to spend the time studying the connection between energy, economy, and the environment. He detected that there was a way to grow the economy by investing in energy efficiency, renewable energy, and other low-carbon solutions. He had cracked the Carbon Code.

Xie now argued with his old colleagues that energy and climate issues were integral parts of the economy and should not be segregated in a new compartment, but should remain with China's preeminent planning agency—the National Development and

Reform Commission (NDRC). NDRC created China's famed "Five Year Plans" and was responsible for ensuring that the goals set forth in them were adequately financed by government and ultimately achieved. He argued that energy was the fundamental building block of any plan and must remain with the NDRC. Xie was allowed to make his case to China's final arbiter, the Communist Party.

At the People's Congress in the spring of 2008, Xie prevailed and the decision was made to leave energy planning with the NDRC—with him as the vice minister in charge. He also persuaded party officials to make climate change a part of his portfolio, given the clear nexus between energy and carbon emissions. With carbon and energy policy under his control, the Chinese economy was effectively his to command. The quiet, studious engineer was now one of the most powerful men in China.

Dim Sum Diplomacy

Over informal buffet-style meals of poached, puffed, and artfully presented foods, the Americans and Chinese at the Commune by the Great Wall tended to kibbitz among themselves in their native tongues. Xie shrewdly began each meal in pleasant chatter with his colleagues over a bowl of soup, but then sat down for a main course with me and the other U.S. delegates. He was a good listener and visibly absorbed information like a sponge. When we returned to the more formal setting of the meeting room, Xie asked even more probing and insightful questions, becoming especially animated when I described what California and other leadership states had done, effectively turning the United States into a Kyoto-compliant nation in spite of the lack of a federal solution.

When it was our hosts' turn to speak, they surprised us with a detailed inventory of transformative measures they were taking to cut carbon, but all under the rubric of energy efficiency measures or renewable energy development initiatives—much like the work of California and the other states. They did not set carbon reduction targets or even issue reports on the nominal reductions achieved from these measures, focusing instead on their goals around getting more productivity out of less fossil fuels.

In fact, starting as early as 2000, China had launched a nation-wide campaign, achieving impressive results in energy efficiency and the development of renewables. Xie's experts clicked off slide after slide—the inefficient power plants and smelters they had closed, equal in energy terms to half of California's entire electrical grid; the building standards they had established that now covered a billion square feet of new construction; the gigawatts of wind, solar, and biomass facilities that were built. Admitting that they were building a new coal-fired power plant every week, they highlighted that this was largely to replace the oldest, dirtiest plants—something the United States was certainly not yet doing. Despite a blizzard of statistics, none of these remarkable accomplishments was described in terms of the carbon emissions avoided.

Why didn't they tell the story with all of these facts and figures converted to describe the carbon benefits? I was told that while China's negotiators didn't want to commit to carbon reductions until the United States did, Xie and his counterparts could actually begin to reduce carbon by making this fundamental shift in how the economy would grow. They could speak the language of the co-benefits for now, because that's how they and their subordinates across the nation were being measured, but no one was yet allowed to focus on carbon.

Knowing this, it became clear that China had more reason to become a low carbon economy than any other nation on earth. To maintain social "harmony," a word much in evidence all across China and code for one-party political rule with no opposition, they needed to provide jobs. Jobs for a growing population come from a growing economy, so the government's goal is 10 percent growth per year. Xie had long ago concluded that there is no way to grow the global energy supply—or China's share of it—by 10 percent per year for very long, which meant the economic growth would have to be based on getting more production from less traditional sources of energy. Thus, China needed to become more energy efficient and switch to domestic renewables as soon as possible—for the sake of "harmony."

Xie also laid out for us the basic differences between China's approach to carbon and that of the developed world, disparities that would need solutions before any new global agreements could be reached. He said that China wanted measurements described per capita instead of total emissions per nation, because China's emissions on that basis were a quarter of America's and highlighted the need for the United States to do much more. Further bolstering that view was the fact that developed nations had used up much of the atmosphere to gain a modern standard of living, so those countries should now be required to mitigate that disproportionate share of the pie-eating contest before China should have to get started. That included meeting the United Nations' "Kyoto" targets—or paying developing nations as a means to avoid making such reductions now—before China or other developing nations should have to change their path to economic development.

Of course some of these demands seemed hollow, given what Xie and his team had told us was already going on in China and why, but the elephant in the room was still the "face" deadlock between China and the United States.

"How," he asked rhetorically, "could our two countries find a path together when our fundamental views remained so far apart?"

"What if our two countries continue to talk about that path," I suggested cautiously, suddenly struck by what seemed too obvious an answer, hesitant to sound foolish and be told my idea was silly. "But our states and your provinces could actually work together on the solutions, sort of a model for our countries to follow in time. Couldn't we even enter into agreements to do the things we hope our nations will do one day—setting carbon reduction targets; reaching mutual agreement about how to measure such reductions; cleantech research and technology exchanges between institutions like California's UC Berkeley and China's Tsinghua University; collaboration on reducing carbon content of things we sell each other like cement or forestry products; and creating carbon credits in China for sale into the new carbon markets we're creating in our states, just like the ones sold into the European market today?"

I waited for uncomfortable coughs or outright snickering, but instead Xie stroked his chin, sat back in his chair and smiled.

"That's a very interesting idea," he said slowly. Even hearing it in Chinese before the translator spoke, I could tell he was measuring each word precisely, knowing that his colleagues were taking notes and that nothing was really off the record. "We could explore that in the future."

Xie rose. The meeting was clearly over. I was pleased by the overall reception to the idea of a "subnational" approach, but concerned that I had just created an international incident that had caused the meeting to end abruptly. Two hours later, to my relief and pleasant surprise, I got a call from Xie's intermediary. He was very impressed by the idea of state-province agreements that could provide a template for our nations. If many of our states and provinces were to cooperate, neither the United States nor China would need to "go first"—because we would already be tackling the climate crisis with practical solutions in our states, provinces, and businesses. I was authorized to report back to "my colleagues"—meaning governors and presidential candidates— that China was willing to engage in this approach.

As summer gave way to fall and the silly season of endless presidential campaigning culminated in an historic election, the states' climate and energy policies began to bear fruit. Because of its head start, California rapidly lowered greenhouse gases by deploying solar, wind, and other renewable energy—20 percent of its total energy supply is now renewables and a third will be by 2020—with alternative fuels like hydrogen-powered cars, and with energy efficiency incentives, making the Golden State 40 percent more energy efficient than the rest of the country.

Other states were seeing the green shoots of similar results and their governors, both Democrats and Republicans amid election year partisan warfare, were reaping political benefits along with economic and environmental ones. Obama was elected and, because he had learned to crack the Carbon Code, U.S. and world climate and energy policy would not wait much longer for a positive change.

In fact, the world waited only two weeks. We asked President-elect Obama to put his stamp on the climate issue at the Governors' Global Climate Summit in Los Angeles that was hosted by Governors Schwarzenegger (CA), Doyle (WI), Gregoire (WA), Napolitano (AZ), and Blagojevich (IL—yes, the same Rod Blagojevich who was forced from office a few weeks later). The goal was to show the world what a group of states, provinces, and other subnational governments had accomplished and to help the new administration and Congress overcome any fear that the challenge was too great.

"The science is clear," Schwarzenegger had said three years earlier when we launched our campaign to lead the United States on carbon solutions. "The debate is over. The time for action is now. California will reduce emissions to their 1990 levels by 2020 and an additional 80 percent by 2050."

Using much the same rhetoric on November 18, 2008, two months prior to being sworn in as the forty-fourth president of the United States, Barack Obama addressed the Governors' Summit.

"The science is beyond dispute," the president-elect said with the now-familiar rhetorical certitude. "The facts are clear. Now is the time to confront this challenge. The United States will reduce emissions to their 1990 levels by 2020 and an additional 80 percent by 2050." In 2009, comprehensive legislation to tackle climate change was passed by the House of Representatives and in 2010 the Senate began to address the issue based on the solutions already being designed and deployed by individual states.

Nor did the new President wait long to engage China. On July 29, 2009, U.S. Secretary of State Hillary Clinton and China's State Councilor Dai Bingguo signed a cooperative agreement on climate change. The agreement called for the creation of specific programs to reduce carbon emissions at the "subnational" level, meaning states and provinces, and paved the way for the deals we had envisioned in the shadow of the Great Wall one year earlier. Standing quietly to one side, witnessing the ceremony at the State Department in Washington DC, was Xie Zhenhua.

In November of 2009, California and Jiangsu province signed the first of those deals at the second Governors' Global Climate Summit in Los Angeles. In addition to a commitment to becoming 20 percent more energy efficient, China had also announced a goal of planting enough new trees to cover an area the size of Norway and to meet 15 percent of its energy needs with renewables, all before 2020 and all in the context of carbon reduction. In late 2009, China launched a new carbon registry aligned with global standards and launched a voluntary carbon market, much like the Chicago Climate Exchange in the United States (a market where U.S. corporations reduce their carbon emissions by buying carbon credits that were created from projects that reduced greenhouse gases in developing countries as described in Appendix C).

Turning Policy Into Profits

As the list of subnational, national, and international regulations, markets, and carbon reduction targets grows and merges, business managers must take action to become more efficient and reduce carbon based on these trends. But how do you begin? How do you afford to make changes in the way you do business, especially in challenging economic times? What is relevant to your business—and when?

The following chapters will answer all of those questions and give you the insights necessary to crack the Carbon Code today and as it evolves from its historical DNA. This information will describe the steps to make almost any business more efficient, sustainable, and competitive in the global economy, and more profitable long into the future.

Sources

"A New Chapter on Climate Change," President-elect Barack Obama, viewed on October 1, 2009 at http://www.youtube.com/watch?v=hvG2XptIEJk&feature=player_embedded.

"California and UK in Climate Pact," BBC, August 1, 2006.

"China Environment Head Steps Down," UPI, December 3, 2005.

"China, U.S. Sign MOU On Energy, Climate Change, Environment Cooperation," July 29, 2009 http://www.fmprc.gov.cn/eng/zxxx/t575904.htm.

China's Clean Revolution, The Climate Group, 2009.

"Chinese voluntary carbon standard launched," Point Carbon, September 23, 2009.

Climate and Energy Roundtable, The Climate Group, July 31, 2006.

Earth Summit, United Nations. http://www.un.org/geninfo/bp/enviro.html accessed October 1, 2009.

"Governor Calls for Curbs on Emissions," *Los Angeles Times*, April 12, 2006.

"Green changes sweep province of B.C.," *Vancouver Sun,* February 15, 2007.

"Let's look beyond the haze;" *Fast Company,* August 1, 2008.

"Never was so much owed by so many to so few," Wikipedia, accessed November 25, 2009.

State Building Blocks, Climate Policy Program, New America Foundation, http://www. newamerica.net/programs/climate; accessed October 1, 2009.

Tamminen, Terry, Sasha Abelson, and Kristina Haddad. *Climate Change Handbook* (Santa Monica: Seventh Generation Advisors Press, 2009).

"The America Price," *Fast Company,* August 29, 2009.

The Climate Group, website accessed September 23, 2009, http://www.theclimategroup.org/index.php?pid=428.

"UN Climate Summit Puts China, India in Spotlight," Associated Press, September 22, 2009.

"Western Governors Adopt Policies on Clean, Diversified Energy, Global Climate Change and Transportation Fuels," Western Governors Association, June 11, 2006.

"Xie Zhenhua bio," http://www.chinavitae.com/biography/87, accessed November 24, 2009.

CHAPTER 2

Cracking the Carbon Code Step One: Time Your Carbon Tipping Point

How can anything survive in a climate like this? A heat wave all year long. A greenhouse effect. Everything is burning up.

> —From the 1973 film *Soylent Green,* more than a decade before the first hearing on climate change in Congress

Contrary to the character's assertion in *Soylent Green*, everything is not burning up. "Climate change" is a better term than "global warming" to describe the phenomena that are playing out on the world stage, due largely to the combustion of fossil fuels, because the increased concentration of greenhouse gases in the atmosphere causes a variety of changes to weather patterns, and not all of those are increases in temperature. Regardless of these trends or the nomenclature used to describe them, they have highlighted an opportunity for businesses to use carbon as a measure of efficiency and, by reducing waste, increase profits. In some cases, the trends also suggest ways to avoid significant liabilities as the impact of climate change alters landscapes and operating environments.

There are five basic steps to cracking the Carbon Code and making your business more profitable, while getting ahead of regulatory trends:

1. Time Your Carbon Tipping Point: Deciphering regulation and business trends that determine when carbon concerns will reach your doorstep.
2. Build a Fence: Measuring your company's carbon "footprint" and deciding what emissions you must accept as part of your responsibility—and which ones are someone else's liability.
3. Cut the Carbon: Reducing your company's carbon emissions in the most cost-effective manner and unlocking hidden "carbon assets" that may generate new revenues.
4. Manage What Can't Be Cut: Mitigating risks associated with a price on carbon, including the secrets to entering the carbon credit markets.
5. Estimate Carbon Resilience: Evaluating the long-term prospects for your company's carbon footprint and learning to adjust accordingly. This step includes understanding benchmarks for continuous improvement by comparing your company's carbon performance against others in the industry—and learning to stay ahead of the pack.

Each of these steps is illustrated in the following chapters with examples of companies that have successfully cracked the Carbon Code and those that are still struggling to master its lessons. Every manager can learn from both, but the most important lesson of this entire book is to get started *now*.

The first step is knowing when the carbon tsunami will come to your shore—timing your Carbon Tipping Point.

The Timing of Your Carbon Tipping Point: Three Questions to Ask

I don't know if Peter Darbee, President and CEO of California's massive investor-owned utility Pacific Gas & Electric (PG&E),

had ever glided through the sky in a cherry picker before, but most certainly I had never done so. Yet there we both were, on the outskirts of Sacramento, California, at the mammoth refrigerated warehouse of Tony's Fine Foods, hovering over thousands of square feet of gleaming new solar panels that had just been installed on the company's roof.

Peter described how he had tracked the reports and rumors about climate change for several years, but, like many Americans, had not been able to distinguish fact from fiction. This uncertainty made it difficult to decide how PG&E should respond, if at all. He commissioned academic experts to summarize the credible science about likely scenarios, especially what the physical impact of climate change would be in PG&E's service territory. He brought his top executives together in a secret retreat to hear the results.

"What they told us made our hair stand on end," he said with a somber intensity. "We could expect significant flooding and erosion in areas with our transmission lines; heat waves that would cause electricity demand to soar; health impacts on our employees. That's just to name a few of the consequences. The experts told us that we could expect these changes much sooner than most were forecasting them."

Like Peter Darbee, many smart business and political leaders had begun to crack the Carbon Code and were convinced that the global economy would not only prosper by adopting low-carbon technologies and policies, but also lower risks and costs. A price on carbon would essentially be a cheap insurance policy. In fact, businesses spend billions each year for insurance to offset risks that are far less likely to impact their bottom line—because it's good risk management. Why wouldn't every business owner do the same to protect against the growing concerns around climate change, much as Peter Darbee was doing?

Of course no business wants to change its operating model or incur new costs ahead of demonstrated need. This first step in cracking the Carbon Code—*timing* your Carbon Tipping Point—will help you decide when your company needs to take carbon-risk-mitigation measures of its own. There are three questions to ask when estimating the timing of your company's Carbon Tipping Point.

When Will My Business or Industry Be Regulated?

Regulations or a direct price on carbon are being imposed in different parts of the world on varying timelines. By tracking developments using the information presented in this book, you will be able to determine when state, federal, or global regulations are likely to apply to any particular industry in any given territory and with what effect.

In the European Union (EU) and thus far in the United States, regulations are aimed at the biggest sources of carbon emissions first. Figure 2.1 shows global sources of carbon in 2007 according to the United Nations' Intergovernmental Panel Climate Change.

Not surprisingly, therefore, regulation has aimed first at electricity production, large industrial facilities, and transportation. In the United States, electricity has been the first target among these major emitters, because in most parts of the nation utilities are regulated monopolies or are owned and operated by municipalities on behalf of ratepayers. As such, they provide an excellent pilot program for regulating carbon, because utilities can pass new costs on to consumers under structured rate programs that are typically controlled by public utility commissions or city councils

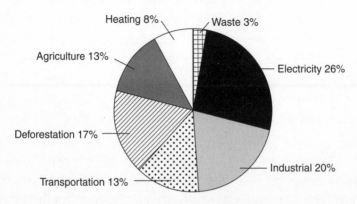

Figure 2.1   Worldwide sources of greenhouse gas emissions in 2007

to prevent sudden rate spikes that might otherwise disadvantage either businesses or low-income consumers.

Regulating any of these sources demands data. Therefore, as part of the Obama administration's use of the Clean Air Act to begin regulating carbon, the U.S. Environmental Protection Agency (USEPA) issued a rule in late 2009 that covers reporting requirements for these major emitters, about 10,000 installations overall (installations that emit 25,000 metric tons or more of CO_2 per year). Most of the reporting is at each installation, but some fossil fuel suppliers report at the corporate level. The first report is due in March 2011 for emissions during calendar year 2010. USEPA estimates that these 10,000 installations cover 85 percent of U.S. emissions.

In addition to those sources that will be regulated first, it is equally useful to note which industries are NOT directly covered by these data-reporting rules—at least not yet:

- Electronics manufacturing and sulfur hexafluoride emissions from electrical equipment
- Oil and natural gas systems
- Ethanol production
- Fluorinated chemical production
- Food processing
- Industrial landfills

Underground coal mines (and suppliers of coal); magnesium production; and wastewater treatment facilities were originally proposed to be exempted, but were since included in the reporting requirements.

After reporting, which emitters will be required to obtain a permit to emit carbon and subsequently be required to reduce those emissions? In early 2010, under the "new source review" provisions of the Clean Air Act, USEPA issued rules for the largest sources that are already operating under a Clean Air Act permit for other pollution emissions and that are adding *new* equipment or significantly modifying existing sources of carbon emissions. These include new installations that emit at least 100,000 tons of carbon annually and remodeled facilities that increase emissions by at least 75,000 tons.

In total, these new permitting rules cover about 70 percent of all carbon emissions from stationary sources, such as coal-fired power plants, cement producers, glass and steel manufacturing, and oil refineries. The rules take effect in January 2011, although landfills and factories not already covered by other Clean Air Act permits, but which emit at least 100,000 tons of carbon annually, would also be required to obtain a permit for these emissions by July 2011. Sources that pollute less than 50,000 tons each year will not be covered until 2016. Under the rules, companies will be required initially to demonstrate that their installations use the "best available technology" (often referred to as "BAT") to cut carbon when building new plants or modifying existing ones.

Again, it is worth noting the categories that are *not* on this regulatory list. Initial proposals for this rulemaking in late 2009, which would have included much smaller sources of carbon emissions, were criticized because expensive technological costs might have been imposed on mom-and-pop businesses such as dry cleaners. In response, when the regulations were finalized, USEPA decided that the rules would not cover carbon emission sources of less than 50,000 tons annually, at least for now (the so-called "tailoring" rule, where the strict requirements of the law are tailored for practicality).

If your business is not covered by any of these rules, you may still feel the impact of the expanding effort to regulate carbon on the same timeline as the major emitters. The supply chain of almost any business runs on energy or depends on the products supplied by installations that are covered by the rules. Costs are likely to be passed on, although, as later chapters describe, the point of reducing carbon is to reduce waste and therefore make businesses more efficient. Those efficiencies can offset added costs imposed on whatever emissions remain after a facility has used the best available technology to reduce its carbon pollution. Either way, as covered installations begin to adjust, there may be changes in supply-chain costs passed along to other businesses that are not themselves the direct subject of carbon limits, at least temporarily.

Another example of carbon regulations that will affect almost every business, directly or in the supply chain in the near future, are the carbon limits on vehicles that were first created in California in 2004 and were adopted by the Obama administration in 2009 to apply nationwide. As secretary of the California EPA at the time, it was my duty to promulgate these new rules in ways that were both cost-effective and technologically feasible to reduce carbon emissions from vehicles. In applying those parameters, we found that the average price of a car would increase about $1500, but the fuel savings would offset that cost in two or three years of typical operation. These rules will affect businesses in two potential ways—purchase prices of vehicles will increase slightly, but fuel costs will drop significantly.

Although the California rules limit the actual carbon emissions from the tailpipes of vehicles, the federal approach is to regulate fuel economy and thereby reduce emissions of all types. Under the new federal rules, cars and light trucks, beginning with the 2012 model year, will be required to achieve a fleet-wide average of 35.5 miles per gallon by 2016, nearly ten miles per gallon better than the current average. In 2010, President Obama ordered the addition of large trucks to the program, which account for only 4 percent of vehicles in the United States but consume as much as 20 percent of the nation's fuel supply. In 2011, the first mileage standards for these trucks will be adopted, applied initially to the 2014 model years. It is interesting to note that passenger cars account for about 33 percent of carbon emissions from the transportation sector; light trucks, such as SUVs, account for about 29 percent; and large trucks account for 21 percent.

Trucks are certainly in the supply chain of most businesses and lighter vehicles are often in corporate fleets. Following California's example, however, in both cases the federal rules seek to achieve fuel economy improvements that are both cost-effective and technologically feasible, so the initial costs that may be added to new vehicles will be rapidly offset by lower operating costs.

When Will Customers Demand That I Deal
with My Company's Carbon Footprint?

Regardless of when government authority limits your company's carbon output, consumers may demand to know—and see evidence of efforts to reduce—your products' carbon footprints. For example, Walmart will soon require a sustainability label on all of the 100,000 products on its shelves, including a carbon footprint—and what company today is not directly or indirectly a part of the Walmart supply chain?

The public also wants this information. Think about Kathie Lee Gifford discovering that kids in sweatshops were manufacturing her clothing line a few years ago. Or consider the nutritional labels on food demanded by consumers long before regulators stepped in. For its standard-setting, Walmart pulled together the best academics from around the world to establish the way they want things measured and reported to them—and their customers. Given Walmart's enormous economic footprint, you can be sure that regulators are watching and learning from these efforts and will make use of any system developed by and for the world's largest retailer.

Moreover, if you make or use packaging, there may be an added focus by regulators and consumers on the embedded carbon in those materials. USEPA estimates that packaging may be directly or indirectly responsible for as much as 40 percent of carbon emissions in the United States, measuring not just materials and energy used in the production of packaging materials, but also carbon emitted for their transport, disposal, and recycling. Packaging materials and shipping components, such as containers and pallets, may cost more in the near term. If your business buys packaging materials from other companies, you may expect the manufacturer of those products to take responsibility for the carbon content, but don't count on the public—or Walmart in the United States, Tesco in the United Kingdom, or Carrefour in France—accepting that logic if the package bears your logo. As noted, these retailers and others are responding to consumer demand for information by requiring sustainability

Figure 2.2   Carbon footprint label on milk (Photo courtesy of Lenka Matulova, The Climate Group)

labels that describe, among other things, the carbon content of products. Consumers, therefore, may judge the carbon content of your products and compare it to that of your competition well before regulations require your company to measure, report, or reduce emissions.

*When Will the Impacts of Climate Change Affect
the Assets or Business Model of My Company?*

The assessment done by PG&E is a great example of a company that saw regulation and consumer interest on the horizon, but also foresaw effects on the company's physical assets. Taken together, it motivated Peter Darbee into action, because he understood that the time of his company's Carbon Tipping Point had already arrived.

Insurance companies provide an interesting indicator for estimating the timing of when climate change impacts may occur to specific businesses, because they must understand the Carbon Tipping Point of every client they insure. As a re-insurance company, Swiss Re evaluates the accuracy of the estimating done by other insurance companies for their clients—the actual businesses that are being regulated and compelled to take action.

"It could change the predictive model," notes Chris Walker, Head of Sustainability Business Development at Swiss Re in

2006. "If we don't have the model right, we could face problems in pricing some business going forward." Put another way, insurance estimators assume that things like fire, flood, drought, human health, and other insurable systems are predictable over the long term, if not always precisely predictable in the near term. Climate change and its consequences change all of that in very unpredictable ways. Swiss Re reports that the entire insurance industry recorded 40 billion dollars of weather-related losses in 2004—the highest figure in history—and the following year, the economic losses for windstorms alone topped 200 billion dollars.

To address this third question more precisely, Swiss Re became a company that funds more climate risk research than most universities and shares it with policymakers as well as with its clients. Of course, by sharing the data it can justify rate increases, but it has also offered rate reductions to insured companies that have taken measures to reduce their own carbon liabilities.

Asking your insurance company may be one of the most direct ways of answering this third fundamental question about a company's Carbon Tipping Point. Other ways include reviewing the location of your company's physical assets and those of your primary customers. Like PG&E, are they in areas that are already flood-prone and where small changes in storm patterns or sea level could result in significant damage and business interruption?

Other climate change–related damage that might increasingly affect a company includes storm damage to buildings; power outages; worker health (especially if a company has workshops or other facilities in warm climates that are not air-conditioned); reduced water supply; altered growing seasons; and invasive species not normally found in your region (a factor that is probably limited to food and agricultural businesses).

Finally, it is important to your business to know risks that may impair your supply chain. Discuss these kinds of exposures to the impact of climate change with your key suppliers and consider defensive strategies, such as increasing inventory (if affordable) or diversifying the source of those critical supplies.

Compare Your Business: Carbon Tipping
Point Winners and Losers

Below are several examples of likely winners and losers that have accurately estimated their Carbon Tipping Point—or failed to do so.

Winners Know Their Carbon Tipping Point

More intense hurricanes and sea level rise have made it clear that the Carbon Tipping Point for insurers in coastal states is already here. When every other insurance company that wrote homeowner policies moved out of the state, Olympus Insurance Company in Florida (www.olympusfl.com) priced the risks of climate change–related disaster into its products and moved in to pick up the business. As noted earlier, Swiss Re (www.swissre.com) and other insurers have moved away from insuring open-ended risk in areas likely to feel the first major impacts of climate change, something that one could argue has already happened in places such as New Orleans after Hurricane Katrina.

In response to carbon reduction policies, governments are regulating the efficiency of products that use energy. As noted, vehicles were among the first to be the subject of that approach. In a similar move, rather than ban inefficient incandescent light bulbs, California lawmakers set an efficiency performance standard—which was then adopted by the federal government—so that in 2012 energy-wasting bulbs won't be for sale in America. Seeing that the Carbon Tipping Point had arrived for some of its products, Phillips (www.lighting.philips.com) developed and marketed its "Halogená Energy Saver" incandescent bulb that is 30 percent more efficient than conventional versions and competes favorably with energy-efficient compact fluorescent and LED bulbs. The performance standard approach—instead of the government picking winners and losers—clearly worked for both environmentally minded policymakers and bottom-line–minded businesses and gave them insights into the timing of their Carbon Tipping Points at the product level.

Think about the energy required to freeze ice cream, transport and store it in freezers at grocery stores, and keep it cold until you're ready to consume it. Consider the carbon emissions associated with that embedded energy. Unilever (www.unilever.com) scientists developed ice cream that can be stored and transported at room temperature. All of that energy—and its related carbon footprint—is reduced to just the energy needed to chill it before serving. Unilever was shrewd enough to see that their Carbon Tipping Point was fast approaching, both because of the pace of regulation and consumer demand. Applying the Carbon Code to everything in its supply chain showed Unilever management that, while their own operations generate about four million tons of carbon emissions per year, the total carbon burden in their products, including all life-cycle parts of the supply chain, brings that total closer to 400 million tons per year. Unilever began reducing the carbon footprint of its own factories, fleet, and offices, but realized that a 20 percent reduction would only cut about 800,000 tons a year, while a meager 5 percent reduction from the supply chain slashes twenty million tons per year—well ahead of their Carbon Tipping Point.

Losers Don't Know Their Carbon Tipping Point

Agriculture is highly dependent on water and growing seasons, but as an industry has done little to prepare for the changes that are already being documented in some of the most productive growing regions of the nation. As a result, companies that serve agribusiness, such as Cargill (www.cargill.com), may also be adversely affected. Nor does Cargill itself appear to be adapting its corporate culture to these inevitable changes. For example, the Cargill "Water Matters" program consists of measures such as trash pickup along the Potomac River and class excursions led by teachers to Cargill facilities in Georgia to learn about water-testing procedures, rather than proactive initiatives to help customers conserve a resource that is being reduced in many parts of the United States by climate change–related droughts.

Similarly, Weyerhaeuser (www.weyerhaeuser.com) and other paper/pulp companies are taking few measures to address their dependency on water, energy, trees, and other natural resources that will soon be threatened by climate change. Moreover, policymakers are increasingly focused on meeting carbon reduction targets with a strategy known as "avoided deforestation." Research shows that large amounts of carbon are released when forests, especially those with dense old growth, are cut down. Scraps from the logging process decompose and other forms of greenhouse gases are released from the disturbed soil. Timber operations will come under growing scrutiny and regulation, which may impact forest products companies that have not understood this imminent Carbon Tipping Point and taken actions to offset their direct and indirect emissions.

Commodities that power cargo planes and delivery vans, such as jet and diesel fuel, take more energy to make than gasoline and, while commuters have choices when gas prices spike, package businesses have no alternatives "when it absolutely, positively has to be there overnight." As a carbon price is added to these fuels, companies like FedEx (www.fedex.com), UPS (www.ups.com), DHL (www.dhl.com), and even the humble Greyhound bus line (www.greyhound.com) will need to reduce their dependence on fossil fuels dramatically to stay profitable. Understanding the timing of that component of their Carbon Tipping Points will be essential to their business models.

In Conclusion

Timing your company's Carbon Tipping Point in various parts of the world can be straightforward if regulations have been adopted, but can also be complicated by the science or the politics surrounding climate change.

For example, New Zealand Prime Minister Helen Clark told me in 2007 that her nation gets almost all of its electricity from hydro power and therefore isn't concerned with emissions from power plants, which is typically the largest carbon source in other countries. New Zealand's emissions come mostly from sheep and cows, which are much harder to regulate. As a result, New Zealand is working on reductions from everything else first, including factories and vehicle emissions, while doing research on animal feeds and digestion to find ways to reduce methane emissions from both ends of their livestock. This demonstrates the idea that each country and industry needs flexibility with its carbon reduction plans—some industries lend themselves to immediate reductions and others just take time!

Of course the exact timing of the Carbon Tipping Point for many companies will remain unclear for some time—even in Europe, many existing carbon regulations officially expire in 2012 and it's not certain what will replace them—but it is quite clear that carbon will soon have a price across the economic spectrum. Smart managers will get ahead of that trend and prepare their company or portfolio, as PG&E did, proactively determining their Carbon Tipping Point by answering the three questions presented in this chapter. Of course these questions cannot be answered without understanding *what* carbon emissions to look for, *where* to look for them, and *what* to report to regulators and the public. That requires Step Two of cracking the Carbon Code: measuring.

Sources

Breaking the Climate Deadlock: Technology for a Low Carbon Future, The Climate Group, 2009.

Brohe, Arnaud, Nick Ere, and Nicholas Howarth. *Carbon Markets: An International Business Guide* (London: Earthscan, 2009).

Business Guide to the Low Carbon Economy, The Climate Group, 2009.

Cargill "Water Matters" program http://www.cargill.com/corporate-responsibility/environmental-innovation/environmental-partners/water-matters/index.jsp, accessed November 23, 2009.

"Europe's Ban on Old-Style Bulbs Begins," *New York Times,* September 1, 2009.

Final Rule: Mandatory Reporting of Greenhouse Gases from Magnesium Production, Underground Coal Mines, Industrial Wastewater Treatment, and Industrial Waste Landfills, USEPA, at http://www.epa.gov/climatechange/emissions/remaining-source-categories.html accessed September 1, 2010.

Final Complementary Policies White Paper, Western Climate Initiative, May 20, 2010.

Hoffman, Andrew J. *Carbon Strategies: How Leading Companies Are Reducing Their Climate Change Footprint* (Ann Arbor: University of Michigan Press, 2007).

"New York Prepares for Era of High Seas," Wall *Street Journal*, September 11, 2009.

"Nine Industries That Are Screwed by Climate Change," *Discover Magazine*, October 3, 2009.

"Phase-out of incandescent light bulbs," Wikipedia, accessed December 22, 2009.

Soylent Green, Metro-Goldwyn-Mayer, 1973.

State Building Blocks, Climate Policy Program, New America Foundation, http://www.newamerica.net/programs/climate, accessed October 1, 2009.

Stolaroff, Joshuah. *Products, Packaging, and U.S. Greenhouse Gas Emissions* (Athens, GA: Product Policy Institute, 2009).

Tamminen, Terry, Sasha Abelson, and Kristina Haddad. *Climate Change Handbook* (Santa Monica: Seventh Generation Advisors Press, 2009).

"The Education of PG&E's Peter Darbee," *San Francisco Chronicle*, October 18, 2006.

"Tony's Fine Foods Solar Installation," Press Release, June 27, 2006, http://www.solardevelop.com/projects.html.

"Unilever Wants Ice Cream to Ease Global Warming," *Times* (London), August 24, 2009.

"U.S. EPA Issues Rules on Biggest Carbon Polluters," Reuters, May 13, 2010.

"Water Use and Conservation," www.weyerhaeuser.com, accessed November 25, 2009.

"West Sac Gets State's Largest Biz Solar Project," *Sacramento Business Journal*, September 5, 2005.

CHAPTER 3
———————

Cracking the Carbon Code Step Two:
Build a Fence

A man who carries a cat by the tail learns things he can learn
in no other way.

—Mark Twain

In the 1950s, government and industry officials said nuclear power
would be so inexpensive, there would be no need to meter it. In
other words, electricity would be free. Imagine that you had built
a business at that time based on this premise, but today the local
nuclear power plant decided to begin charging for electricity after
all. You would look at your company through a very different lens,
adjusting to an increase in a cost of production that was as significant to your bottom line as it was unexpected. Electricity-hungry
businesses would suddenly be worth much less than those that
put a premium on efficiency or used their own sources of renewable energy such as solar and wind power. Stock values would be
revised over time as charges for electricity mounted. Many previous darlings of Wall Street would be dogs, and vice versa.

As we now know, nuclear power was actually very expensive, so electricity was never given away for free. In a similar vein, however, our atmosphere *was* given away for free, but as described in chapter 2, there will soon be a price for every business and consumer, based on their proportional emission of carbon—a price that *may* be significant to one's bottom line, but certainly need not be *unexpected*.

Having determined the timing of when the carbon price will be added to an industry, its Carbon Tipping Point, savvy businesses next need to measure how much carbon they emit to know their potential liability and just how much to adjust business plans. Companies that are heavily dependent on energy from fossil fuels will find that a price on carbon, through regulation or the cap-and-trade systems being developed across the United States, are worth much less than those with a smaller carbon footprint. Energy and resource efficiency will be king—but how can you know what regulators will demand, or what the relative efficiency of competitors in an industry will be, without measuring?

Some intuitive forms of measuring have been at work for a while, but so far they have mostly remained invisible. Investing in Toyota a few years ago, for example, turns out to have been smarter than buying GM stock, in no small measure because Toyota and its Prius used carbon-based fuels more efficiently than GM and its Hummer. Makers of compact fluorescent light bulbs (CFLs) are literally turning the lights out on makers of incandescent bulbs, as many states and countries ban inefficient lights for the same reasons, and continued low-carbon innovation will soon see LED lights outshine the CFLs.

A growing number of companies are measuring their carbon footprints, an exercise that can indicate which companies may be hurt by paying for something that has thus far been free, or illuminate those that can *benefit* from low-carbon technologies and regulations. The hidden cost of carbon, or benefits to the companies that reduce it, increasingly becomes obvious as regulations are imposed, but can be forecast by unlocking the secrets of the Carbon Code beforehand, which starts by acquiring reliable, practical data.

You Can't Manage What You Don't Measure—The Three Carbon Metrics

There is an old saying that good fences make good neighbors. Measuring your company's carbon footprint is first and foremost an exercise in defining your fenceline—what is your responsibility and what is your neighbor's. In this chapter, you will learn how and what to measure using three basic principles.

1. The Carbon Footprint: determining the specific carbon emissions that regulators and consumers expect will be your responsibility.
2. The Carbon Yardstick: the measuring system itself, which you can use to arrive at specific numbers for your annual carbon footprint or for the products you sell.
3. The Carbon Registry: the places where you can publicly record your carbon footprint to comply with both government regulations and public expectations.

Carbon Metric #1: How Big Is Your Carbon Footprint?

Imagine you own Bob's Bakery. The carbon emissions from the gas oven that bakes the pastries are clearly a part of your carbon footprint. So are the emissions from the oil-fueled boiler that generates heat to keep your factory warm on a cold winter's morning and the emissions from the natural gas-fueled water heater on your property. You also own a large fleet of trucks that deliver the baked goods each day; the diesel fuel you burn in the trucks is your responsibility, as are any fugitive emissions from vents or leaks on the diesel fuel tanks on your property. These *direct* emissions, caused at and by your business activity, are called Scope 1 emissions.

Scope 1 emissions are relatively easy to measure, because you control the machinery and pay the fuel bills. On the other hand, Scope 2 emissions (also called *indirect* emissions) are those that are generated by someone else, but clearly on your behalf. The power plant in your city is likely responsible for the emissions related to the electricity generated to light your bakery, but you know from your monthly electric bills how much of that burden is actually attributable to you.

Scope 3 (also called *optional*) are emissions created by someone else—and likely to be someone else's responsibility—but from which you derive benefit: air travel by your national bagel sales force, for example, and the carbon footprint of the waste disposal from those dumpsters behind the Bob's Bakery installations. The carbon needed to manufacture the plastic bags used to package the bagels certainly belongs to the company that supplies them to you, but what about the fuel used to ship those heavy cartons of plastic bags to your facility?

Determining the extent of your fenceline for each Scope can be tricky, or a matter of corporate responsibility policies, but there are at least two tests that offer guidance about what should be in or out—the equity share approach and the control approach. As "equity share" implies, if you own part of an activity that causes carbon emissions, you would include that percentage in your carbon footprint. For example, if a delivery truck brings your bagels and another bakery's bread to the same grocery store, each company would accept a proportional share of the carbon responsibility for the fuel. On the other hand, if the truck is loaded only with your products, you "control" that source of emissions and would include 100 percent of it in your calculations.

Another way to approach the equity versus control issue is to look at revenue. For example, the U.K. grocery chain Tesco demands that a carton of milk display a carbon footprint label. What if the dairy got 75 percent of its revenue from selling milk and 25 percent from selling meat and leather? Tesco would say allocate 75 percent of the dairy's carbon emissions to the milk and the rest to the other products.

Bagels and milk provide an interesting look at specific products from a company, but how do you determine the fenceline of an entire industry? For example, consider cement, one of the largest sources of carbon emissions globally in the industrial sector. Cement is the component in concrete that binds together the sand

and gravel into the final product that is poured for foundations and a host of other familiar uses. Over 100 cement plants in the United States produce about 85 million metric tons of cement each year, but the plants are only part of the carbon emissions genealogy. The production of cement involves four steps, each of which results in significant carbon emissions and each of which may be inside one company's fenceline or another:

- Extraction of the raw materials, such as limestone, clay, or pumice.
- Refining the raw materials, which involves blending the raw materials into a powder.
- Converting the powder to "clinker" by heating it to more than 2,500°F in a kiln.
- Mixing the clinker with other ingredients, such as gypsum or fly ash from coal-fired power plants, to produce the actual cement product.

In measuring the carbon content of a cement plant, therefore, regulators must decide if the focus should be on the final product (cement) or the key component (clinker) in its manufacture. A measurement based on clinker production may incentivize process improvements and greater kiln efficiency, but one based on cement might cause manufacturers to avoid a carbon cost by importing clinker from a region where emissions are not regulated and thereby avoid reflecting the true carbon footprint of the final product. This phenomenon is called "leakage," meaning that the source of emissions simply "leaks" to another jurisdiction, giving the appearance of reduced carbon in one territory, but actually increasing emissions in another.

Regulators are carefully looking for those unintended consequences and companies should not hope to avoid carbon regulation for long by simply shifting the burden elsewhere. Establishing an honest fenceline and taking steps to reduce carbon ahead of regulations will make better business sense in the long run, because changes in production or cost structures can be anticipated rather than reacted to.

John Chambers, the chairman and CEO of Cisco Systems, came to visit Governor Schwarzenegger in 2005 and surprised us by saying his company was already beginning to measure its carbon footprint. As a company without smokestacks, he shrewdly built a fenceline that accepted responsibility for Cisco's obvious Scope 1 and Scope 2 emissions (based on electricity and fuel bills from leased and owned facilities), but publicly pushed Scope 3 sources outside its fenceline. He figured out what would pass a reasonable observer's smell test by seeking advice from the Carbon Disclosure Project, a nonprofit organization that helped Cisco refine its data collection and reporting, but also helped to justify what was kept outside its fenceline. "Why would Cisco publicly report carbon emissions when no regulator has asked you to do that?" Schwarzenegger asked Chambers as we sat around the massive oak conference table in the Reagan Cabinet Room in Sacramento. "As a high-tech company, we feel obliged to be ahead of the game, especially when we can use new information technology to do it," Chambers said proudly, eager to tell the best part of the story. "And..." he paused for effect, "we save money by doing it. We'll save over a million dollars this year on energy costs by reducing our carbon footprint—something we might not have done had we not been measuring."

Chambers described how he came to realize that you can only manage what you measure. Measuring carbon helped Cisco discover that 80 percent of the company's direct energy bills were paid to cool the computers and servers in 50 office buildings and research labs. This motivated Cisco engineers to redesign its products to produce less heat, saving money on energy used to power the devices and on the air conditioning of the rooms in which they were operating. This in turn led the way to new Cisco products that were more valuable to its customers.

Next, Chambers brought in interior designers to create more flexible work spaces that allowed more natural air flow and used less energy from forced cooling and heating. By looking for ways to reduce its carbon footprint even further, Cisco discovered the financial benefits of using state and federal incentives to get nearly 10 percent of its energy from solar and other renewables.

Finally, when Chambers decided to take responsibility for things such as employee air travel in Cisco's Scope 3 carbon measurements, he not only found another way to cut both cost and carbon, but realized there was growing demand for yet another new product that would help Cisco's clients. The videoconferencing technology "Telepresence" was born and has since grown to be a significant revenue source for the company. By jumping into the measuring game early, Cisco was able to reduce its own carbon footprint, save money, and improve its products. It also helped the company to stake out valuable territory—by accepting responsibility for no more than will likely be necessary under future carbon regulations.

Cisco learned how to be a good corporate citizen and improve the bottom line in the process, but whether you manage Bob's Bakery or a multibillion-dollar IT firm, it can be tricky to decide exactly *how* to measure. If your business operates in Europe, there are existing standards for what's in and what's out of these scopes, and government standards that set rules for how to measure and report. Because regulation in the United States is still emerging, the yardsticks and goalposts are just beginning to be defined. So what system should you use in the United States, and who can reliably make your measurements?

Carbon Metric #2: Choosing a Carbon Yardstick

Once a company determines what is inside and outside its carbon fenceline, the actual method for measuring Scope 1 and 2 emissions will be obvious, typically just by using fuel and electricity bills along with generally accepted methods of calculating emissions from those fuel sources in your region. Scope 3 carbon, however, will likely be much harder to measure and will be a matter of what you choose to include. If you include your employee air travel, for example, you won't have access to the airline's fuel bills, so you can only estimate the carbon footprint of each trip using generally accepted standards (see the Resource Guide for companies and nonprofit organizations that have developed widely accepted tools to help you make the calculations for all three Scopes).

Whether your business has engineers to conduct in-house measurements or uses a contractor, the key to success is choosing a measuring and reporting system that is recognized by existing regulatory schemes (such as the EU ETS or RGGI) and will likely be recognized by emerging systems (such as California's AB32 and WCI). Although there are several options, one standard that is generally accepted at this point is the Greenhouse Gas Protocol (GHGP), designed by the World Resources Institute (WRI). The other generally accepted standard comes from the International Standards Organization (ISO) and is based on the GHGP. The ISO standard for carbon measuring is labeled ISO 14064.

Measuring is done differently for different types of sources, but all of these systems are based on standards created by the GHGP. An installation with a smokestack, such as a power plant, is easy to measure because exhaust gases have been sampled and measured for some time under other air quality regulations. Other emissions are harder to measure at the source, such as tailpipe emissions from a fleet of delivery vehicles. In that case, generally accepted models are used to extrapolate emissions data from the fuel and engine types used.

Similarly, electricity bills can be used after determining the type of generation (for example, an electricity bill with a certain number of kilowatt hours consumed from a coal-fired utility will have a larger carbon footprint than one from a utility with hydro or natural gas power plants). Fuel bills can be used after determining the type of on-site machinery that uses the fuel (water heaters using natural gas or building heating systems using fuel oil, for example).

Of course verification of data is crucial to acceptance, now or in the future by regulators, and to avoid criticisms of "greenwashing" from consumers. Contractors, including several nonprofits, such as those described in the Resource Guide at the end of the book, are used for such verifications, much like hiring a financial auditor.

Having decided what to include in your initial carbon footprint measurement, using widely accepted protocols and standards such as GHGP, the installation (or the entire company) now has a "baseline" year against which future carbon reductions can be measured. Kyoto Protocol nations use 1990 as the baseline year, but you may not have data going back that far (GHGP simply recommends going back to the year with the most reliable data). The farther back you can go (and the more you can show reductions from business-as-usual) the more valuable the data will be in terms of monetizing any carbon reductions you make going forward.

Of course businesses grow and contract over time, so there is a need to update emissions data annually, which may be tricky if your daily, hourly, or seasonal output is variable. Remember, you are responsible for annual emissions, so that's the measurement that needs to be measured and reported, regardless of how things change from day to day in your operations.

So far this chapter has addressed nominal measurements, either actual calculations from sampling data or extrapolation based on fuel usage, to arrive at a specific number of tons of carbon emitted, which is the least controversial method of determining a carbon footprint and its changes over time. However, the nominal approach may not be the most advantageous to your business, be generally accepted in your industry, or conform to some future regulatory schemes. Therefore, there is another way to describe a facility's carbon footprint—by measuring carbon intensity.

The concept behind carbon intensity (also called "carbon benchmarking") is that a growing business (or a rapidly developing nation such as China) should not be penalized for success. Regulations may set a cap on emissions from the Scope 1 sources at Bob's Bagels, for example, but what if Bob suddenly gets a new customer and doubles the output of his bakery, despite successful efforts to make his equipment more efficient and convert part of his energy supply to renewables? In this case, Bob would advocate for regulations based on carbon intensity rather than just the nominal value of total emissions from his bakery. Using that approach, Bob would be measured by the carbon intensity of his products—what is the carbon output of every 1,000 bagels, for example? The calculation would look like this:

Emissions (expressed in tons of CO_2e)

Units of output (XX thousand bagels) = Carbon intensity (per thousand bagels)

Businesses like Bob's, or countries like China under international agreements, would rather be measured on their efforts to reduce the carbon intensity than the total nominal emissions. Regulators are also warming to this approach, because it allows for shifts in the marketplace and avoids costly fights over fairness. If Bob and his competitor, Betty's Bagels, start out with about the same market share and carbon footprint, regulators would put the same cap on their emissions and mandate the same reductions each year. But if Bob loses market share to Betty, she will have problems meeting her obligations, while Bob may have a windfall of carbon credits to sell as his emissions decline well below the cap in proportion to the decline in production. The carbon intensity measurement would be more fair and easier to regulate.

Understanding this critical concept of the Carbon Code allows you to advocate for the yardstick that is most advantageous to your business while regulations are still being designed. In California, state officials established a Market Advisory Committee to consider these very issues and similar opportunities to influence the initial design of the system are available in the regional cap-and-trade systems (WCI and RGGI, for example, as described in more detail in chapter 5 and Appendix C) and will be part of any federal rulemaking in the future under standard provisions of the Clean Air Act.

Smart companies engage early in these opportunities, but can only make informed and potentially profitable recommendations based on having calculated their carbon footprint well ahead of regulations being finalized. Cosmetics giant Avon, for example, reports reducing its carbon emissions over 30 percent between 2002 and 2008 based on per unit measurements, while Proctor & Gamble achieved 52 percent cuts per unit of production in a similar time frame. The Clorox Company has set a goal of reducing its emissions 10 percent per case of product sold by 2013 (against a baseline year of 2007). Ford Motor Company reports an overall carbon reduction of 45 percent between 2000 and 2008, plus emissions reductions per vehicle of 24 percent over the same period.

Large companies have state and federal lobbyists who can get their clients engaged in these opportunities, but what if you are Bob or Betty and have enough work to do to keep up with local bagel marketing and don't have that kind of costly representation? Numerous trade associations are getting into the carbon advocacy game, both helping their members to share carbon-cutting strategies and technologies, but also to participate in the regulatory process. Because this field is still in its earliest days in the United States, participating through a trade association is a cost-effective way to protect your business interests and to keep up with rapidly changing developments. Another approach is to get information from trade associations in your industry in Europe, where the regulation of carbon (and experience with cost-effective ways to reduce a carbon footprint) are about five years ahead of the United States

Having built a fence and chosen a yardstick, the final Carbon Metric involves a place to report the data so that shareholders, government regulators, the public, and customers (including sustainability-oriented customers in your sales or supply chain, such as Walmart) have access to it. That's where a "registry" comes in.

Carbon Metric #3: Keep Score—Choosing
a Carbon Registry

In 2000 I was managing the Environment Now Foundation in Los Angeles and got a call from the Secretary of the California Resources Agency, Mary Nichols. She asked if the foundation would make a small grant to pay for the creation of a new climate change-related nonprofit organization that would somehow engage companies in the battle to deal with greenhouse gas emissions. As a favor to a friend, I agreed to take the call from Mary's colleague, Diane Wittenberg.

"We're calling it the California Climate Action Registry," Diane told me. "Companies will measure their carbon output and announce it to the world by registering the data with us." "Why would they do that?" I asked, also wondering who would care if they did. Remember that in 2000, few people in the United States cared about climate change and indeed the Kyoto Protocol was still four years away from ratification. I respected Diane because of her work with electric vehicles at Southern California Edison, but I must admit I wasn't astute enough to discern the forward-thinking wisdom of her vision for this registry thing. "Well, at first, maybe no one will do it," she said with her customary candor. "But certainly no one *can* do it if there's no place to register. I think we can get a few to start us off and over time more will join."

When I hung up the phone, to be honest, I still didn't understand what I was funding, but a few thousand dollars for legal work to form a nonprofit that might be meaningful in the future, on a topic of growing environmental importance, seemed a reasonable investment. Little did I know, although Diane certainly understood, what a giant harvest would come from planting these few meager seeds.

"The Climate Registry is a coalition of U.S. states, Canadian provinces, Mexican states, and Indian tribes that have come together to support a single greenhouse gas reporting and accounting standard," Diane told a reporter in 2008, when her California program had evolved into an international hub for measuring and publicly reporting carbon emissions that both governments and corporations were using. "You can look at a parallel in financial accounting standards. The problem that needs to be solved is consistency in the very simple underpinnings and infrastructure of measuring carbon emissions. If one state measures one way and another measures another way, they don't trust one another's data. Companies have really pushed them hard to have consistent reporting, and the federal government hasn't been leading that effort, so the states have come into the void and provided their own leadership."

Today, The Climate Registry (TCR) has evolved from a California institution to the place where USEPA and government at all levels accomplish that goal—clear, consistent, reliable measuring and reporting of carbon emissions. As both state and federal regulations are developed, we now know where to look to understand precisely what is being regulated. The Climate Registry accepts data measured using the GHGP and makes it easy to report data collected by its members using a standardized web-based reporting system called the Climate Registry Information System (CRIS) (which is based on one created by the original California organization, called the Climate Action Registry Reporting Online Tool or "CARROT").

Registries are to carbon what the county recorder's office is to real estate transactions. Those like TCR not only ensure proper accounting and reporting of carbon emissions, but also that any reductions are properly recorded and carbon "credits" from such reductions are not counted more than once. They provide another useful service as your company gets into the measurement process, providing accreditation for consultants and protocols to make those choices easier.

As the third aspect of establishing a company's carbon fenceline, registries play a crucial role in creating a reliable, transparent foundation for both regulation and a carbon market. Some registries are privately operated and, because carbon credits are property rights (essentially the right to use a portion of the atmosphere to deposit your installation's carbon), traditional contractual transactions can also serve the purpose of establishing this foundation. The Resource Guide lists other Registries and forms of recording a company's carbon footprint and its efforts to reduce it.

So Just What Is My Carbon Shoe Size?

Having gone through all of this analysis and reporting, what will a typical carbon footprint report look like?

Anthony Minite appears to be a humble, soft-spoken next-door-neighbor type—you wouldn't guess he was an ecorevolutionary and a masterful CEO with hundreds of employees. When he showed me around his Bentley Prince Street (BPS) carpet factory in the City of Industry, California, in October 2007, I was experiencing massive cognitive dissonance. After nearly two decades of environmental activism, including a stint as a government regulator, I was used to large manufacturers complaining about onerous environmental rules and the impossibility of keeping jobs in the United States against competition from other countries that imposed no such costly obligations. But around every corner of Minite's massive factory, I saw solid evidence to the contrary, and listened to him brag about the cost savings of doing things green.

"We use less water, less toxic stuff, and generate almost no waste," he said matter-of-factly, with an air that assumed any smart CEO would be making carpets the same way. "And check this out—the biggest solar array of any business in North America!" We stepped outside and saw a typical industrial storage yard, but this one was covered in gleaming solar panels. Installed more than a decade earlier, the panels had already paid for themselves. Minite was able to gloat that his company now enjoyed about half of its electricity for free.

"This also really cut our carbon footprint," he added, too humble to point out that he had made his company the first charter member of the California Climate Action Registry and one of only two manufacturers in the state to measure and register a carbon footprint so early. BPS and its parent company, Interface, had gone on to lower their carbon footprints, making their products among the most sustainable in the floor-covering industry, saving tens of millions of dollars, and slashing waste they send to landfills by 81 percent. Water use per unit of output dropped by 36 percent and other air pollutants had fallen by 35 percent.

So after all of these efforts, what does BPS's carbon footprint look like? Thanks to good data, pro-active measuring, and recording results with a respected registry, the company was able to record a 50 percent reduction of its carbon footprint within ten years, reporting along the way as Table 3.1 describes.

Table 3.1 Annual carbon emissions report: Bentley Prince Street, from California operations

**Verified Emissions
Information**

Reporting Year:	2006
Reporting Protocol:	General Reporting Protocol, Version 2.2 (March 2007)
Baseline Year (Direct Emissions):	2002
Baseline Year (Indirect Emissions):	2002

Direct Emissions	CO_2e	CO_2	CH_4	N_2O	HFCs	PFCs	SFs	Unit
Mobile Combustion:	**44.94**	44.26	0.00	0.00	0.00	0.00	0.00	metricton
Stationary Combustion:	**8,424.04**	8,399.88	0.94	0.01	0.00	0.00	0.00	metricton
Process Emissions:	**0.00**	0.00	0.00	0.00	0.00	0.00	0.00	
Fugitive Emissions:	**0.00**	0.00	0.00	0.00	0.00	0.00	0.00	
TOTAL DIRECT:	**8,468.98**	8,444.13	0.94	0.02	0.00	0.00	0.00	metricton

Indirect Emissions	CO_2e	CO_2	CH_4	N_2O				Unit
Purchased Electricity:	**2,638.13**	2,633.91	0.02	0.01				metricton
Purchased Steam:	**0.00**	0.00	0.00	0.00				
Purchased Heating & Cooling:	**0.00**	0.00	0.00	0.00				
TOTAL INDIRECT:	**2,638.13**	2,633.91	0.02	0.01				metricton

Compare Your Business: Carbon Footprint Winners and Losers

By measuring and registering ahead of regulation, BPS can not only charge more for the "green" attributes of its products in the marketplace, but the company will also be eligible to apply to regulators for "early action credits" that it can use during future compliance periods or sell to others (more on that in subsequent chapters). Other carbon footprint winners and losers include:

*Winners: Those Who Measured
Their Carbon Footprint*

The most obvious winners for measuring carbon footprints are the measurers themselves, firms such as PE International (www. pe-consulting-group.com) in Germany, or Natural Logic (www. natlogic.com) in the United States. Engineering firms are adding this skill to their offerings and will also prosper, including large firms such as Ameresco (www.ameresco.com) and CH2M Hill (www.ch2m.com). Big companies are hiring their own teams, so anyone with an engineering degree may find a new and valuable application for his/her skill, especially in the bleak job markets of the recent recession.

One reason to measure a carbon footprint is to uncover hidden sources of carbon, revealing the long-term winners and losers. Oil from tar sands in Alberta or highly polluting refineries in Saudi Arabia will soon have a higher carbon footprint label on every barrel. By contrast, the Abu Dhabi National Oil Company (www.ADNOC.ae) is building its new massive refinery project with the strictest pollution control systems available, to make the refined product that is measurably lower in carbon content and, therefore, more valuable to carbon-conscious consumers in the EU and United States. The carbon content in fuels has already become an issue in states like California (and Congress has indicated support for this approach nationwide). The California Low Carbon Fuels Standard (LCFS) requires that fuel providers lower the total carbon content of all fuels they sell in the state on average. This means a company selling gasoline or diesel fuel can reduce the overall carbon by blending biofuels, reducing the emissions at the refinery, selling non-carbon fuels such as hydrogen, or investing in battery-charging stations or any other means of achieving reductions on a portfolio basis. Because of this policy, the carbon content of oil brought into the state for refining will partly determine the ability of the fuel provider to meet this standard.

One of the most dramatic examples of the benefits of measuring the carbon footprint of everything in the supply chain can be found at iGPS (www.igps.net), a maker of plastic shipping pallets. Because its pallets are about a third lighter than their wooden counterparts, the fuel savings from shipping is obvious and so is the lower carbon footprint. Moreover, wood pallets consume vast tracts of forest every year, something unsustainable in a literal sense as global demand outstrips supply, and forests are being protected by the worldwide effort to avoid deforestation to prevent more greenhouse gas pollution. The plastic pallet doesn't require toxic fumigation or extra trips to the repair station, something that also reduces the overall carbon footprint. Bottom line? If you had measured the carbon footprint and other life-cycle resource inputs to these two competing products in 2007, you would have predicted that iGPS would capture a big/growing chunk of the market and that CHEP (www.chep.com), the wooden pallet monopoly, would lose over six billion dollars in market cap as customers and retailers shifted to plastic pallets—exactly what happened by 2009. By the way, Walmart gives companies that ship on iGPS plastic pallets extra points on its packaging scorecard over those that still use wood because of the lower carbon footprint and broad sustainability values.

Losers: Those Who Failed to Measure
Their Carbon Footprint

Although not yet required to measure their own carbon footprints, coal carriers are already losing business because everyone else is measuring theirs. Dakota, Minnesota & Eastern Railroad (www.dmerail.com) has been working on a coal line from Montana and Wyoming to power plants in the East for more than a decade, and walked away from the project when it became clear that the demand was declining for the product they would be carrying and banks refused to finance the risky project—one that had seemed like a sure thing when it was started in 1997. Other major U.S. coal railways are also likely to be losers—Norfolk Southern (www.nscorp.com), Burlington Northern Santa Fe Railway (www.BNSF.com), CSX (www.csx.com), and Union Pacific (www.up.com), which get up to a fifth of their revenues from hauling coal.

As noted above, CHEP (www.chep.com) and other makers of wooden shipping pallets will soon be sent to the same commercial ash heap as the makers of buggy whips and gas lamps. Look through your company to find other wood, cardboard, and heavy paper products that may soon be replaced by lighter alternatives because of carbon and resource-depletion considerations. Similarly, many companies are replacing heavy steel components in products or the supply chain with aluminum, especially recycled aluminum which contains as much as 90 percent less embedded energy than virgin materials.

Mutual funds that are heavily invested in companies with large, immovable carbon footprints are certainly at risk too. In 2009, the most carbon-intensive funds were:

- iShares FTSE/Xinhua China 25 Index Fund (http://us.ishares. com) at 1,549 tons of carbon per million dollars in revenue (FYI, the most carbon efficient funds hover around 50 tons per million dollars);
- Fidelity Capital Appreciation Fund (http://content.members. fidelity.com) at about 758 tons per million; and
- Janus Fund (www.janus.com) at around 744 tons per million.

In Conclusion

Whether examining the specific carbon footprint of your company or analyzing specific products, you will want to publicize the findings to stake your fenceline territory against others and to send the message to Wall Street that you're ahead of this liability. Of course, if the measuring shows that your carbon footprint is large and growing, move ASAP to the third step of cracking the Carbon Code—cutting your carbon footprint.

Sources

Bayon, Ricardo, Amanda Hawn, and Katherine Hamilton.*Voluntary Carbon Markets* (London: Earthscan 2009).

"Big Coal Carriers Navigate a Risky Climate Track" *New York Times,* September 16, 2009.

Business Guide to the Low Carbon Economy, The Climate Group, 2009.

Carbon Disclosure Leadership Index 2008, Carbon Disclosure Project, www.cdproject. net, accessed January 4, 2010.

"Carbon Intensive Mutual Funds to Become Big Losers," *ClimateBiz,* April 8, 2009.

Cisco Corporate Citizenship Report, Cisco Systems, Inc., 2005.

"Do an Hour on the Lifecycle," *Fast Company,* January 16, 2009.

"Hate Calculus? Try Counting Cow Carbon," *Wall Street Journal,* September 18, 2009.

"Hot Job: Calculating Products' Pollution," *Wall Street Journal,* September 1, 2009.

"Governor Schwarzenegger Announces Environmental and Economic Honors," California *Ensuring Offset Quality: Design and Implementation Criteria for a High-Quality Offset Program*, Three Regions Offset Working Group, May 2010.

GEELA Awards, Environmental Protection Agency, Bentley Prince Street, December 1, 2004.

"Greenhouse Gas Emissions from Alberta Oilsands Higher than Some Countries," *The Canadian Press,* September 13, 2009.

Issues and Options for Benchmarking Industrial GHG Emissions, Stockholm Environment Institute, May 12, 2010.

Lewis L. Strauss, speaking of nuclear energy to the National Association of Science Writers in 1954, said "It is not too much to expect that our children will enjoy in their homes electrical energy too cheap to meter."

"Nine Industries That Are Screwed by Climate Change," *Discover* magazine, October 3, 2009.

Notable Member Accomplishments & Goals, Reported 2009–2010, Corporate Eco Forum, June 8, 2010.

"North American Jurisdictions Coalesce around the Climate Registry's Carbon Reporting Standards," interview with Diane Wittenberg, *VerdeXchange News* vol. 1, no. 11: March/April 2008.

"Oil Sands Stocks Directory," Investorideas.com, accessed October 1, 2009.

Portland Cement Association (http://www.cement.org/)

"Refiners Target Countries with Lax Environmental Laws," *The National*, July 4, 2009.

CHAPTER 4

Cracking the Carbon Code Step Three: Cut the Carbon

Rule No. 1: Never lose money.
Rule No. 2: Never forget rule No. 1.

—Warren Buffet

The invitation was of the most pedestrian design, standard-issue business conference stuff, but one name in italics caught my eye: *His Serene Highness, Prince Albert of Monaco.* A roundtable discussion about alternative-fueled vehicles and green buildings, hosted by the London-based nonprofit The Climate Group, presumably to help the prince green up the Ferraris and castles of Monaco.

The event was being held in the fall of 2009 in association with United Nations week in New York, a year with a particular emphasis on the solutions for climate change. We were waiting for President Obama to finish speaking to the General Assembly that day, so the prince could sneak out of whatever serves as a back door at the UN and get to this meeting of cleantech investors, CEOs, and advocates. I stood talking with Clay Nesler, a

VP at Johnson Controls, who told me what sounded like a green fairy tale.

"So every night, we take 50 windows out of the walls," he said, referring to a retrofit project at the iconic Empire State Building, being performed by Johnson Controls, Serious Materials, and several other green products companies. "We replace them with windows that were rebuilt during the day. There's a team in a workshop on the fifth floor that renovates them with triple insulation, special gases, and films that make them more energy efficient. It'll take about nine months to do all 6500 of them."

"Sounds expensive," I said, looking out over a dull gray New York cityscape from the twenty-third floor of the midtown office high-rise.

"Not really, because the payback is only three years from energy savings," Clay answered with a salesman's enthusiasm at being asked his favorite question. "We're installing controls on lights and heating and cooling to reduce energy when each room is not in use. And we're sticking insulation between radiators and old brick walls. Do you realize that 60 percent of the heat was going through the walls, so the Empire State Building has been heating all of New York City, instead of its tenants, for years?"

As I quizzed him for more facts, right up to the moment we were introduced to the late-arriving Serene Highness, I learned that the building would save almost 40 percent of the energy it had been using, and that they could have saved twice that much if the building owner had been willing to do things with five or six-year paybacks. The other obstacles to making the building more efficient were the tenants themselves—especially lawyers— who refused to move as much as a desk without compensation, so all of the work had to be done in stealth mode.

What the Empire State Building story demonstrates is that there are many cost-effective ways to cut carbon after you know your carbon footprint. The first things to consider are energy-efficiency products, process improvements, and renewable energy that actually pay for themselves, then work your way toward the things that cost more.

Wouldn't it be great if there were a handy checklist that helped you consider each carbon-reducing measure in terms of cost-benefit priority? Many companies have blundered into expensive replacement technologies or purchased carbon offsets because they didn't have such a list to consult. In fact, such a list exists and will make your life much easier as the carbon manager for your firm. This largely overlooked "secret" list is found in something called the McKinsey Curve.

Money in the Cushions: The Law of Carbon Gravity

In July 2009, an energy expert working for the international consulting firm McKinsey & Company stood before reporters at the National Press Club in Washington DC to draw attention to an astonishing discovery. He and his team had spent years studying energy use in America and, no matter how many times they scrubbed the numbers or reviewed them with peers, they kept arriving at the same startling conclusion.

Ken Ostrowski learned to sniff out waste as an intern at the Congressional Budget Office before applying his knowledge at General Electric and finally McKinsey. He toiled for years in the firm's electric and natural gas practice where he began to see a trend that alarmed him. Any engineer knew that energy was lost in the form of heat from things such as inefficient light bulbs or car engines, but he suspected that the volume and value of wasted energy—which could easily be saved—was much greater than anyone imagined. As the world grappled with natural resource depletion and climate change, what would it be worth to capture some of that value and put it back into the American economy?

Ostrowski persuaded McKinsey to let him pull a team together that included engineer Jon Creyts, a relative newcomer to McKinsey who had previously worked in Lockheed's secretive "Skunkworks" facility in California (birthplace of the U2 spy plane) and who now headed up the firm's "lean operational improvement" program for power-generating stations. They were joined by Scott Nyquist, who had worked for Exxon before

joining McKinsey in 1984, ultimately to run their energy practice. Nyquist was an out-of-the-box thinker who proposed reducing fuel consumption by allowing megatrucks on U.S. roads, for
example, suggesting that fewer and larger trucks were more efficient than more and smaller ones.

With several other contributors, Ostrowski's team began
researching the question of energy efficiency in 2005, collaborat-
ing with other academics, businesses, and nonprofits. In 2007 they
released the first report that shocked the business and public policy
world, proving that about half of all necessary carbon reductions
could be achieved using technologies that paid for themselves in a
few years, leaving billions of dollars a year in the pockets of consumers and companies thereafter. After two more years of digging
even deeper into the numbers, Ostrowski stepped up to the mic
at the Press Club that warm summer day in 2009 and made his
astonishing announcement about the way America does business
today—and the imperative to crack the Carbon Code and break
the cycle of business-as-usual.

"If we do nothing, we will waste $1.2 trillion of energy," he
said, as each reporter asked the one sitting in the next chair if they
had heard the same figure. Yes, by 2020 we will throw away more
money than was spent on the Iraq War. More money than the
cost of the new U.S. health care program. We will waste approximately $4,000 for every man, woman, and child in America.
"How much [of that waste] gets captured will be decided by policymakers and business leaders," Ostrowski added, emphasizing
that knowing is very different from doing. His team had studied
650 technologies that were more efficient than current ones and
some twenty thousand "micro-segments" of energy uses, focusing solely on off-the-shelf products and services. Those familiar
lights overhead, the comforting hum of the air conditioner, the
windows we take entirely for granted as we daydream, looking
at the landscape outside—all of them will pick four grand per
person out of our pockets and drain a king's ransom from the
national economy by 2020.

Moreover, Ostrowski told reporters that to save $1.2 trillion,
we needed to invest about $500 billion to upgrade our energy

hogs, repaying that cost in about five years from lower energy bills. Such an investment would create jobs in the United States making and installing new equipment, so the beneficial ripple effect as people are re-employed and tax revenue to states and the federal treasury increases is many times greater. Government costs go down as unemployment benefits decrease. That win-win investment would cut our energy use by almost a quarter and reduce our carbon emissions by more than one gigaton. In other words, we could solve a recession and global warming with money we were on a path to waste.

As the significance of Ostrowski's work sank in, policymakers and smart business leaders studied the measures that the McKinsey research had identified as the most cost-effective. Which ones make the most sense for a given region or company depends on how energy is generated and consumed. Ostrowski provided a quick-start guide to help investors and managers figure this out for themselves without having to wade through the 650 technologies or 20,000 energy uses that his team had considered. The secrets were in plain sight in a chart known as the McKinsey Curve. For those who use it, the experience is like finding money in the seat cushions.

As the McKinsey Curve shows, the biggest savings are found by looking at measures with "negative cost." Just as the law of gravity brings physical things down to earth, the Law of Carbon Gravity states that the measures whose costs are the lowest to implement will be the most effective at lowering carbon sooner. Three rules for business clearly emerge when applying the Law of Carbon Gravity: invest in energy efficiency; switch to renewables; and look on the floor.

The First Rule of Carbon Gravity:
Invest in Energy Efficiency

As figure 4.1 shows, this updated version of the McKinsey Curve looks ahead to 2030 and describes energy savings in terms of the reduction in carbon as well as non-energy related GHG reduction

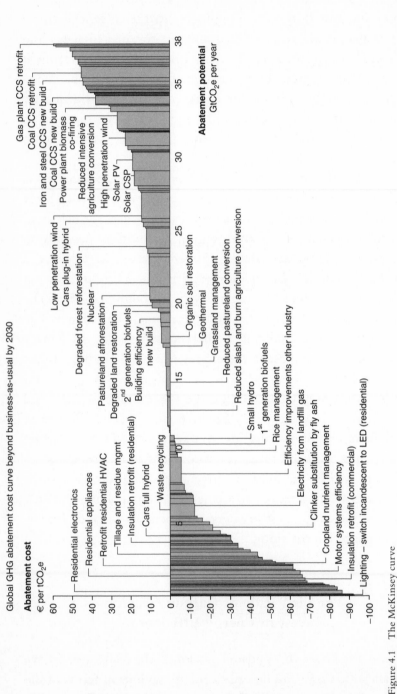

Figure 4.1 The McKinsey curve

Note: The curve presents an estimate of the maximum potential of all technical GHG abatement measures below €60 per tCO₂e if each one was pursued aggressively. It is not a forecast of what role different abatement measures and technologies will play.

Source: McKinsey & Company: Pathways to a Low-Carbon Economy—Version 2 of the Global Greenhouse Gas Abatement Cost Curve.

opportunities. The cost savings in this version of the curve are described in terms of euros per ton of reduced carbon, but the same dynamics exist in the built environment and energy sectors of the United States, China, or any other part of the world. Measures on the left side of the curve have negative cost; in other words, they are paid for by saving money on energy bills. Measures on the right side cost more than they save, but are ranked from left to right in terms of effectiveness on a cost-per-ton of carbon-reduced basis. The greatest savings are in:

- lighting (switching from incandescent to LEDs). Figure 4.1 makes the distinction between residential and commercial, not because these measures only apply to one sector or the other, but because McKinsey estimated where the greatest savings could be harvested first;
- motor efficiency, such as controls on factory equipment or a department store escalator to adjust energy input based on loading rather than simply the on/off switch;
- appliances, which include computer servers, copiers, and other office equipment;
- and something as simple as building insulation, such as the barriers installed between radiators and brick walls at the Empire State Building.

Note too that on the transportation side, hybrid vehicles (both passenger and heavy-duty) can be a cost-effective strategy that can be applied to corporate fleets. As the McKinsey Curve shows, the passenger vehicle sector in particular provides a great example of the benefits of careful analysis. All things considered, plug-in hybrids (which have gasoline engines, but can be run solely on their battery-powered electric motor for short trips) cost more than pure hybrids (which run mostly on their gasoline engine, but are assisted by a battery-powered electric motor), but may not reduce carbon more efficiently, so therefore may not be worth the added cost. Another revelation on the curve is the fact that first-generation biofuels (especially biodiesel made from recycled fats and vegetable oils) are more cost-effective than second-generation (those made from cellulosic materials and crops such as switch grass) but have lower abatement per gallon of biofuel. Hence, second generation biofuels can reach more emission reductions in absolute terms than first generation biofuels. When contracting for lower carbon fuels, be sure to do the math on all options in a given region to ensure the most carbon reductions for the least cost.

The Second Rule of Carbon Gravity: Switch to Renewables

Renewables, such as solar and wind power, sit on the right side of the curve, so may not be the first place you would look for cost-effective measures to cut carbon. McKinsey evaluated only the actual costs, however, exclusive of rebates, tax breaks, or other incentives that can cut the initial cost of some renewables dramatically and place them farther to the left of the curve. In California, for example, the combination of state, federal, and utility company incentives can cut the cost of solar in half. Other benefits may make it worth raising renewables on the priority list too. For example, the large solar array installed by Bentley Prince Street (BPS), as described in chapter 3, provides the company with fixed energy costs for 25 years or more, instead of being at the mercy of rising costs for fossil fuel generation provided by utilities.

Note also the far right side of the curve—"CCS" stands for "carbon capture and storage (also called "sequestration")" expensive technology that will soon be added to conventional fossil-fueled power sources to cut carbon emissions. These costs will be amortized over every electron the utility sells from such power plants, meaning electric bills for those customers are sure to rise significantly in the coming years, another reason to cut the line from a fossil-fueled utility by switching to your own renewable energy generation.

Installation of renewable energy generation ensures that the factory keeps running when grids are strained during hot summer afternoons and blackouts occur. Finally, it gives the company a potentially valuable arbitrage opportunity—carpets at BPS can be manufactured at night, using cheap grid power, and the company's solar power can be sold to the grid during the day, when utilities will pay top dollar.

Combining the first two rules of Carbon Gravity makes even more sense. The four-decades-old Willis (formerly Sears) Tower in Chicago, the tallest building in North America, retrofitted the building's 16,000 windows, 104 elevators, and 15 escalators, and added energy-efficient mechanical and lighting systems. Unlike many other upgrade projects, however, Willis Tower added solar hot-water panels and roof-mounted wind turbines. The result? The building cut the fossil-fueled energy demand 80 percent. That's not a typo—80 percent of the building's energy use was either eliminated or replaced with efficiency upgrades and renewables. The project not only will pay for itself in a few years from those savings, but the lower operating costs make the building instantly worth tens of millions of dollars more, because office complexes sell for multiples of net revenues. Building owners may not always be able to raise rents or occupancy rates, but cutting expenses—especially a line-item reduction of 80 percent—improves the net value immediately.

These projects prepare for another low-carbon technology that will become more important in the coming years—battery-run electric cars. One barrier to battery cars is the added strain on the electrical grid as all those cars charge up. The Willis Tower has reduced its grid energy use by 80 percent, freeing up significant capacity to install charging stations in its parking garages without the local utility needing to add any new capacity. That makes the real estate even more valuable.

The Third Rule of Carbon Gravity: Look on the Floor

In 2005, Walmart brass directed their fleet managers to cut the cost of operating company trucks in half within ten years. There was no evidence that any fleet so large, diverse, and spread across such a large geographical area could accomplish such a dramatic reduction in costs, but Chris Sultemeier, Walmart's senior VP of transportation, got to work to figure out how to do it.

The more Sultemeier looked for ways to save costs, the more he found that the greatest opportunities were in the largest single cost of fleet operation—fuel. To cut fuel use, he improved maintenance procedures (When was the last time you tuned up your car?), driving techniques (setting speed limits and prohibiting jack-rabbit acceleration, for example), and put nitrogen in tires instead of air.

Nitrogen in tires instead of air? From the time you ride your first bike you learn that air leaks from pressurized tires. Nitrogen doesn't leak so easily, meaning the tires remain at their optimal shape longer, reducing rolling resistance and therefore improving fuel economy. Lighter loads are a more obvious way to save fuel, so less packaging or lighter plastic pallets (instead of heavy wooden ones) will reduce carbon emissions and save money. Walmart has implemented all of these steps.

Package delivery companies have realized that idling wastes fuel and generates excess carbon emissions, so routes are optimized with computers and GPS devices to eliminate things such as left turns against traffic, even if the route is made slightly longer, because tests show that those tactics reduce fuel consumption overall. Manufacturers are also learning that their products may be held responsible for a pro rata share of carbon emissions from port activities and are therefore encouraging port complexes to cut carbon, and in some cases are moving their shipping to other ports entirely.

In 2007, I attended a meeting with CEOs and outgoing British Prime Minister Tony Blair at Number 10 Downing Street, where James Murdoch described how a cable provider in his media conglomerate was able to offset almost its entire carbon footprint by replacing inefficient cable television boxes with newer, more efficient ones. Because the company operates in Europe, where a price on carbon was already established, the savings on carbon paid for the technology replacement. Better still, Murdoch explained, he gained the added benefit of customers whose newer devices could provide more entertainment content, and generate more revenues for the company. A switch to newer technology that would have taken years was done in months, because Murdoch had cracked the Carbon Code and found a way to pay for it immediately while simultaneously reducing the size of his carbon footprint.

Another reason to look at what policy wonks call "complementary measures" is that you might find incentives or other programs of value to your company for a variety of reasons. Regulators are giving incentives for things such as workforce training (new skills that teach how to install vehicle charging stations, for example, or training in other services related to the low-carbon economy that may be of value to your company generally); net metering rules (meaning that any solar or other renewable energy you generate must be purchased by the local utility, thus creating a potential revenue source); and installing combined heat and power (CHP) systems.

Because up to two-thirds of energy is wasted in the United States through conversion of fuel to electricity and line losses, CHP may be among the lowest hanging fruit in terms of harvesting a wasted asset that can reduce both carbon and cost. The most basic CHP systems capture waste heat from electricity generation or factory machinery and use it for something productive, such as heating water. This process also eliminates line losses, because the captured energy eliminates the need to send more electricity down the grid to a facility, making this resource even more efficient. As a result, some states provide carbon credits for the reduced carbon emissions from both the captured energy and the efficiency improvement. CHP systems can be economically designed for a wide variety of applications using simple heat exchangers, steam turbines, or fuel cells. Although the majority of CHP systems have been designed for industrial facilities, recent advances in the technology make them applicable to almost any location with a heat source that would otherwise have been vented into the atmosphere, including air conditioners in commercial buildings and homes.

Compare Your Business: Carbon Gravity Winners and Losers

Every day we hear examples of companies that are applying the laws of carbon gravity and cutting their footprint in unique ways.

Coca-Cola, for example, figured out that it could reduce carbon by replacing old vending machines with more energy-efficient models. It can be instructive to any business to stay informed about the results of such initiatives to find approaches that may work in their situation. State regulators may be the best resource for updates on the most cost-effective programs, because they will validate early adopters, confirm metrics used to demonstrate success, and are motivated to see carbon-cutting programs replicated elsewhere to advance their policy goals. Trade associations and nonprofit policy organizations are also good sources and are listed in the Resource Guide. More carbon-cutting winners and losers include:

Winners: Those Who Applied the Rules of Carbon Gravity

Energy-efficiency control companies such as Johnson Controls (www.johnsoncontrols.com), Comverge (www.comverge.com), and EnerNOC (www.enernoc.com) are helping businesses find that money in the cushions and are growing in the process. One way to find examples from other companies, even competitors, that may provide insights for your business, is to look at these consultants' roster of clients and to review their websites and publications.

Energy-efficient lighting will be a major part of carbon-cutting efforts, because items such as LED lights are positioned on the far left side of the McKinsey Curve. Lighting Science Group (www. lsgc.com) is the one to watch, because it has the technology and price breakthroughs that are far ahead of the competition—so far ahead, in fact, that several of the major lighting brands are licensing the technology from Lighting Science to make their own LED products.

Alternative energy suppliers such as Hydrogen Energy (www. hydrogenenergy.com), an innovative collaboration between British Petroleum and Rio Tinto that takes hydrogen from any carbon feedstock (natural gas, petroleum coke, oil) and burns it for clean electricity production. The emission from the process is carbon, but the CO_2 is pumped into depleted oil formations in order to recover more petroleum from domestic sources in the United States and Europe. Carbon is reduced twice—burning hydrogen is cleaner than burning the original carbon fuel, while obtaining oil from sources closer to home saves transportation energy, cost, and carbon.

Losers: Those Who Failed to Apply the Rules of Carbon Gravity

High carbon transportation fuels, such as corn-based ethanol and tar sands, can't reduce the carbon footprint of their products in any meaningful way. In fact, the carbon content of these fuels is increasing over time and will therefore increase the carbon footprint of businesses that depend on them. As the price on carbon becomes clearer, companies such as Blacksands Petroleum (www.blacksandspetroleum.com) and Canadian Oil Sands Trust (www.cos-trust.com) will be in trouble. Corn ethanol producers Renew Energy (www.renewenergyllc.com), Northeast Biofuels, and VeraSun have already taken their investors to bankruptcy court as it became clear that their products would only make the carbon problem worse (despite massive government subsidies and mandates).

Another industry that can't reduce its carbon footprint much is meat production, especially beef. The UN reports that the meat industry generates close to 20 percent of global carbon emissions, mostly nitrous oxide from cow manure and the methane in cow belching and farting. The carbon footprint from growing corn to feed beef adds still more carbon, and the transportation of heavy animals adds even more. Consumers are moving to chicken or fish, which are less carbon-intensive (and eating more vegetarian meals), so producers such as Harris Ranch (www.harrisranchbeef.com) and S&S Meats (www.steaksanywhere.com) may need to diversify both product lines and image if they want to survive in a carbon-constrained world.

Airlines with old fleets will be in trouble—Northwest/Delta (www.delta.com) and American Airlines (www.aa.com) have the oldest, most gas-guzzling fleets in the sky. It will take time to convert these aging assets to more fuel-efficient models.

In Conclusion

The participants in that 2009 conversation with His Serene Highness provided one case study after another demonstrating the application of the Three Rules of Carbon Gravity to effectively cut carbon footprints. As the meeting concluded, I found myself gazing across the gray New York skyline and realizing that there were hundreds of opportunities to do what the Empire State Building and Willis Tower had done. What business opportunities there would be for those smart enough to crack the Carbon Code and get started?

Famed investor Warren Buffett's fundamental rule of successful business is "never lose money." Spending more money than necessary on energy is bad business for both fiscal and carbon reasons. Of course wasteful carbon liabilities in a business can only be cut so far. At some point, there will be a need to manage the remaining carbon footprint. There are very expensive ways to do that, and ways that may cost little or even generate net revenues. That's the fourth step in cracking the Carbon Code.

Sources

"Brazil Takes More Control of Oil Fields, With Long-Term Risks," *New York Times*, August 18, 2009.

Breaking the Climate Deadlock: Technology for a Low Carbon Future, The Climate Group, 2009.

Business Guide to the Low Carbon Economy, The Climate Group, 2009.

"California Fights Shipping Pollution As International Shippers Push Back," *Los Angeles Times*, September 4, 2009.

Coca-Cola 2008 Corporate Responsibility and Sustainability Report, Coca-Cola Enterprises, 2009.

"Energy Efficiency and Demand Response Companies to Watch," *Climate Change Business Journal*, August 19, 2009.

Final Complementary Policies White Paper, Western Climate Initiative, May 20, 2010.

"Greenhouse Gas Emissions from Alberta Oilsands Higher Than Some Countries," *The Canadian Press*, September 13, 2009.

Hoffman, Andrew J. *Carbon Strategies: How Leading Companies Are Reducing Their Climate Change Footprint* (Ann Arbor: University of Michigan Press, 2007).

"McKinsey Says U.S. Energy Use Could Be Cut 23 Percent by 2020," *Cleantech*, July 29, 2009.

"McKinsey: The Next Oil Shock," www.marcgunther.com, March 23, 2009.

"Nine Industries That Are Screwed by Climate Change," *Discover* magazine, October 3, 2009.

Personal communication with Clay Nesler, VP of Johnson Controls, September 23, 2009.

Oil Sands Stocks Directory, Investorideas.com, accessed October 1, 2009.

"Our Destructive Ways," *Sunday Star Times,* August 23, 2009.

Pathways to a low-carbon economy—Version 2 of the global greenhouse gas abatement cost curve, McKinsey & Company, 2009.

Reducing U.S. Greenhouse Gas Emissions: How Much at What Cost? U.S. Greenhouse Gas Abatement Mapping Initiative, Executive Report, McKinsey & Co., December 2007.

"Rival Ports Join Forces on Green Growth," *Los Angeles Times,* December 25, 2007.

"Sears Tower to Undergo Historic Green Retrofit," CoStar Group, June 28, 2009.

Shipley, Anna, Anne Hampson, Bruce Hedman, Patti Garland, and Paul Bautista, *Combined Heat and Power: Effective Energy Solutions for a Sustainable Future,* Oak Ridge National Laboratory, Dec. 1, 2008, at http://www1.eere.energy.gov/industry/distributedenergy/pdfs/chp_report_12-08.pdf.

Smart 2020, The Climate Group, 2009.

Tamminen, Terry, "What's Happening on the Fifth Floor?" *Grist,* September 28, 2009.

"The America Price," *Fast Company,* August 29, 2009.

The National Academies Summit on America's Energy Future, The National Academies, March 13, 2008.

"Wal-Mart Estimates 50% of Fleet Efficiency Gain by 2015 Could Come from Vehicle Technology, 50% from Operational Improvement," Green Car Congress, February 6, 2009.

"Washington Approves Oil-Sands Pipeline," *Financial Times,* August 21, 2009.

CHAPTER 5

Cracking the Carbon Code Step Four: Manage What Can't Be Cut

All mankind is divided into three classes: those that are immovable, those that are movable, and those that move.

—Ben Franklin

Once upon a time, Democrats and Republicans in the United States generally agreed on environmental matters. Democrats were just as responsible for pollution in American rivers that burned with fire, and Republicans could take equal credit for passing laws that tackled air pollution.

By the 1980s, bipartisan laws were protecting endangered plants and animals, slashing air pollution from cars and smokestacks, protecting rivers, and preserving open spaces. One of the most vexing problems that remained unsolved was sulfur dioxide emissions (SO_2) from power plants that were creating acid rainfall, eating away at everything from pine trees to historic monuments. Divided over the cost of abatement—and over who should pay— politicians hunkered down in increasingly partisan bunkers.

Meanwhile, a modest rowing enthusiast named Fred Krupp had just taken the helm of the equally modest Environmental Defense Fund, an upstart Washington DC–based nonprofit group of scientists with a lawyer who had helped ban the use of the pesticide DDT in the United States (yes, the same agro-toxin that Rachel Carson warned about in *Silent Spring*). He spent long nights poring over musty law books, letters from his membership, and his own notes cobbled together from random thoughts during speeches at tedious conferences. There must be a way, he felt, to tame acid rain before it destroyed more of the natural and human-made environment than we could afford to sacrifice.

Across town, Harvard-educated Clayland Boyden Gray spent his days serving in the U.S. Marine Corps Reserve and scrutinizing regulations that his boss and his boss's boss—Vice President George H.W. Bush and President Ronald Reagan, respectively—thought were too onerous on businesses and should be scrapped. Gray was a conservative heir to a tobacco fortune who had gone into public service while still driving an old Chevy he had altered to run on methanol. He cared about the environment, but wanted the marketplace to find the cheapest ways to fix things.

At the end of his eight years in office, President Reagan and his allies in Congress had killed more than five dozen acid-rain-solution bills, prompting Prime Minister Brian Mulroney to humorously suggest that Canada should declare war on the United States to end the invasion of American pollution into his country. As environmentalists lined up behind Democrats and chambers of commerce lined up behind Republicans, exacerbating partisan divisions on environmental policy, Vice President Bush was elected president in 1988, and took Gray with him as legal counsel. Krupp was among the few environmentalists who saw opportunity.

Krupp's nocturnal research had uncovered the work of the early-twentieth-century British economist Arthur Pigou, who argued that many products don't reflect their true costs, especially environmental ones. A polluting factory doesn't pay for the health care of the residents downwind, for example, but taxpayers or health insurance companies do. Pigou suggested that the shareholders and customers should pay such "externalities" through taxes or fees. In 1968, University of Toronto economist John Dales expanded on Pigou's idea, suggesting the hidden costs be paid using a market like the stock exchange.

The basic idea behind Dales's "cap-and-trade" system is that government imposes a cap on emissions of a given pollutant. Each source of these emissions (let's call them "installations") must obtain an "allowance" for each ton of pollution it puts into the air, which collectively add up to no more than the cap. If one installation can reduce emissions below its share of that cap, it can sell the resulting "credits" to an installation that exceeds its share. As long as the total cap is not exceeded, each installation can spend money to reduce pollution or buy credits from another installation that has done so, typically choosing whichever option is cheaper and thereby harnessing the power of the marketplace.

Each year, installations buy and "surrender" the amount of allowances equal to their share of the total cap. And each year, government reduces the cap to get improvements in air quality, but companies can continue to make the cost/benefit decision around cleaning up their own installations or buying dispensations that are the result of another company doing so at theirs. In such a musical-chairs approach, the environment wins and externalities are internalized into the price of the products of each installation at the most competitive cost.

Krupp called Gray at the White House and suggested they work together to create a cap on SO_2 and form a market of allowances that would give businesses the ability to tame acid rain in the most cost-effective manner. He described a bill his staff had already drafted that could amend the federal Clean Air Act and put all of this into motion. We'll never know if Gray was more worried about a Canadian invasion or the growing public outrage over the consequences of acid rain, but he admitted that the market approach appealed to him, and the two got to work.

In 1990, Congress passed major revisions to the Clean Air Act, including a cap-and-trade system for SO_2 allowances. At first, everyone was skeptical. Polluters feared allowance prices could skyrocket and they would be saddled with unmanageable costs.

Environmentalists feared the system could be gamed and no real reductions would occur. Civil rights groups worried that poor people, often minorities, who lived downstream of an installation that bought credits instead of cleaning itself up would pollute more and subject its neighbors to more cases of asthma. Democrats didn't like it because some Republicans did, and vice versa.

After years of rulemaking and design, the system took effect in 1995. SO_2 quickly dropped by three million tons and acid rain levels dropped 65 percent compared to the peak pollution in 1976—achieving the program's goal well ahead of the 2010 deadline. USEPA calculated the overall costs of the program to be less than $2 billion a year, a quarter of original estimates. The internalizing of the cost may sound like a lot, until you realize the external costs that SO_2 had imposed on the rest of us, which was estimated at around $125 billion per year in health care, dead trees, polluted water, and other burdens, a stunning validation of the economic effectiveness of the cap-and-trade marketplace. This market approach also worked to eliminate lead in gasoline, and governments from California to Europe believed it could also prove effective as part of a comprehensive strategy to reduce carbon in the most cost-effective manner.

How does a business get into this emerging marketplace for carbon and use it to meet its obligations? There are three ways to manage your company's carbon footprint by "leasing the sky."

Manage Your Carbon Footprint: Three
Ways To Lease the Sky

Step Four of cracking the Carbon Code is about managing the liability that remains after making all efforts to reduce the carbon emissions of a business. When governments regulate carbon, as they do today in Europe and among power producers in the ten Northeastern states within the Regional Greenhouse Gas Initiative, an installation must pay for every ton of carbon emitted each year. A permit is issued to emit that ton, essentially a new property right that a company owns allowing it to use a piece of the atmosphere to store a ton of carbon.

Managing your carbon footprint can be done with a combination of these three options for "leasing" a piece of the sky:

1. Buying Allowances: Buying the right to use a portion of the atmosphere for one year.
2. Buying Offsets: Paying someone else to give you their right to use a portion of the atmosphere for one year.
3. Playing the Market: Hedging your bets may make economic sense, as allowances and offsets cost a predictable amount today, but may cost much more in the future.

Lease the Sky Option 1: Buy Allowances

Obtaining the right to use part of the atmosphere to store your carbon creates a new form of property right. You acquire that property right, called an "allowance" in one of two primary ways.

First, allowances can be granted by the regulator at no cost. The reason for doing so is to make companies aware of their carbon footprint and to begin the accounting process, understanding that there will be a price sooner or later for the privilege of using that portion of the atmosphere, even if it is free the first year or two. The second way of obtaining an allowance is to buy it, either from the regulator or from another installation that owns more such permits that it needs to cover its actual emissions.

Remember Bob's Bakery from chapter 3? Assume Bob operates in only one state for now, and let's say that in, for instance, New York, regulators have informed Bob that in the first three years of carbon regulation of his industry—the first commitment period—his installation will be allowed to emit 1,000 tons of carbon per year. In the second three-year commitment period, he will have to cut those emissions to 900 tons per year. The limits of 1,000 tons now and 900 tons later are Bob's allocation under the total state cap on carbon emissions.

Bob has done his inventory and was surprised to learn that his bakery and its related emissions totaled 1,500 tons per year.

He took various measures to reduce the number to 1,150 tons, but can't get below that figure without changing his equipment or making other capital investments that he can't afford right away. The state won't sell permits in excess of the total cap it has placed on all installations including Bob's, but will allow him to buy permits ("allowances") equal to his share of the total—1,000 tons—at a state-sponsored auction. New York will use the proceeds to offset higher fuel bills for low-income residents, invest in renewable energy projects, or otherwise use the proceeds of the auction to reduce carbon. After buying the allowances, he "surrenders" them to state regulators as evidence that he has paid for his rental of the atmosphere for that year.

For the other 150 tons his installation emits, Bob has two choices. He can buy allowances from other companies that bought them but ultimately didn't need them (because their emissions were less than their allocation and they purchased the entire amount anyway), or he can buy offsets as described in Option 2.

Some states may give the allocation to each installation in the first few years of carbon regulation to get the system up and running, while avoiding dramatic increases in the cost of doing business. In that case, Bob would have been given 1,000 allowances for free but would still have to purchase the other 150. Some states will give away half in the first commitment period, but require installations to buy the other half. Many experts recommend that 90 percent be given away in the first three-year commitment period, and 10 percent be purchased to encourage some effort at carbon reductions; then 50–50 in the second three-year period; then 100 percent purchased after that. Such a gradual approach is favored by many economists to avoid sudden shocks to the economy, but to incentivize real carbon reductions at every regulated installation over time.

Regardless of the percent of allocation or auction, once a market is created, the price of allowances will be set by supply and demand. Offsets (explained in Option 2) will be priced to compete with tradable allowances, because companies will only buy a credit that offsets carbon emissions elsewhere if it is cheaper than buying an allowance within the regulated system itself. In Europe, for example, allowances have sold for as low as 15 euros and as high as 60, while offset credits that can be used for compliance purposes within the EU typically sell for 20 percent less. In the voluntary carbon markets in the United States and elsewhere, offset credits are valued based on the perceived integrity of the underlying carbon-reducing project. For example, projects that plant trees to absorb carbon in developing countries have sold for less (per ton of purported carbon reduction) than projects to destroy methane from landfills, because the latter is typically easier to validate than the former. Voluntary credits have sold in the past decade for as low as a few dollars per ton to as high as 30 dollars per ton.

Of course the secret to keeping all types of carbon credits competitively priced is the size of the market itself. The larger the number of covered installations, the more appetite for carbon allowances or offsets. Therefore, the emerging carbon markets in the United States (RGGI, WCI, and MGGRA, as described in Appendix C) began in 2010 to synchronize their systems and link them to the EU ETS. It is anticipated the carbon market will therefore become truly global in scope after 2012 (when current commitment periods expire and the newer markets are activated).

Lease the Sky Option 2: Buy Offsets

Like many celebrities, actor and businessman Arnold Schwarzenegger flew on private jets for much of his career. When he became Governor Schwarzenegger, he continued the practice but became aware of the carbon footprint and wanted to do something about it.

Netjets is the world's largest operator of private aircraft. Its founder, Richard Santulli, was a hard-nosed New Jersey businessman who noticed that, even after Europe imposed a cost on carbon, his business there was growing faster than ever. It hadn't affected the bottom line, but had helped Europe become more energy efficient and climate friendly, something his well-heeled clientele on both sides of the Atlantic increasingly wanted to achieve. He pulled together a team of experts to help Netjets reduce the carbon footprint of its operations and invested in research at Princeton and UC Berkeley to invent biofuels that would work safely on jet aircraft. As the world's largest private buyer of jet engines, he began working with GE and other manufacturers to devise jets that were almost half as gas-guzzling as their predecessors. Netjets worked with pilots and the FAA to change airport operations, approach patterns, and flight speeds in order to improve fuel economy and reduce carbon emissions, something that even the major carriers hadn't done yet.

The carbon footprint left over after these reduction measures was divided by each flight mile and customers were given the opportunity to buy carbon-reduction measures from projects around the world, mostly in China, to offset the emissions for each flight. Netjets customers bought these "offsets" as quickly as they were offered—including Governor Arnold Schwarzenegger.

"Wait a minute," the governor said with growing irritation as we advised him of the new Netjets offset program. "I'm the Governor of California, not China. Why are all of these offset things over there? Are there no tons of carbon to reduce in my state? And by the way, how do we know that this place in China actually reduced anything? If it is here, I can be sure of what I'm buying!"

Shifting uneasily in our chairs, we realized that Schwarzenegger had hit on two real issues for offset programs such as these. No one was regulating Netjets at the time, so the program was voluntary. As a result, there were no geographic restrictions imposed by anyone as to where the carbon reductions were achieved—as long as carbon was truly kept out of the atmosphere. The designers of Netjets' offset proposal were sent back to the drawing board to add domestic programs to the mix of carbon-reducing projects, so the governor of California could offset the carbon emissions from his travel with carbon reductions at projects in the United States, especially in California. This would be an important factor in creating offset programs for the regulated carbon markets of the future.

The second point that the governor raised was also important to formal carbon reduction strategies as much as to these voluntary programs. Regardless of geography, how could we confirm that the offset we purchased had actually prevented a ton of carbon from being deposited in the sky?

The basic principle of offsets is simple. Carbon pollution has no greater or lesser effect on the planet, or its inhabitants, if it is released into the atmosphere in one location versus another. Just as American companies manufacture products in places like China because it is cheaper than doing so domestically, it may be more cost-effective to pay an installation in China to reduce carbon emissions than to do it at a U.S. factory, landfill, coal mine, or other source of carbon pollution. United Nations policymakers and regulators in Europe therefore created the Clean Development Mechanism (CDM) to facilitate just such a program and to encourage economic growth in emerging economies which were less dependent on fossil fuels.

Under CDM (and a companion program called Joint Implementation, or JI, which applies mostly to Russia and states of the former Soviet Union), an entrepreneur can capture escaping methane from a coal mine in China and either destroy that greenhouse gas or use it for generating electricity that would be cleaner than coal-fired power. The resulting reduction in tons of CO2 will be certified by auditing firms (which are authorized by the UN), and these carbon offset credits will then be sold to a company in Europe that needs reductions. Details of how these programs work can be found in Appendices B and C and are relevant to the global carbon market, because U.S. and other regulators are adopting variations on these strategies.

In fact, while something less than 20 percent of an installation's carbon reductions in Europe can be achieved through offsets such as CDM, U.S. regulators favor allowing up to half of an American installation's emission reductions to be met using these less costly methods. Just as lower-cost manufacturing in developing nations creates more competition in the marketplace, allowing a greater percentage of carbon offsets from these countries should create competition to lower carbon-cutting costs domestically.

Offsets offer another advantage: they are sold at a fixed price and can lock in a company's cost of compliance. Commitment periods, typically three years, allow you to demonstrate compliance for the entire period. Some risk managers wait until the end of the three years to see how their installations are doing with actual carbon reductions (Why buy credits of any kind if you are reducing the carbon footprint itself?) or because they believe offsets and other credits may be cheaper in the future. If that risk is unacceptable, offsets purchased today at a known price are a better bet.

During the first few years of CDM offset buying/selling, problems arose because of "additionality." Inherent in Schwarzenegger's concern about getting what you pay for, is the question of whether the carbon reduction would have happened anyway. It's clear that a solar panel installed on a rooftop, in response to an incentive payment that cuts the cost in half and therefore allows the owner to repay the net cost in five years, for example, is a project that would reduce carbon without any further mandate or payment. That project is therefore not "additional" to what would have occurred under a business-as-usual scenario. There are a few other ways to prove additionality, including whether the project helps to commercialize new technology faster than would have occurred otherwise, but the financial test is the most commonly applied.

CDM credits therefore must be additional. There are several ways to prove additionality, but the simplest is to show that the carbon-reducing project would not have been economically feasible without the added payment for carbon credits. In the case of Netjets and the governor's desire to do something domestically, that led to installing solar panels on community centers and schools, which would not have happened without Netjets' paying for the resulting carbon credits. Although the California Solar Schools project is voluntary, it demonstrates what regulators will look for in future regulated markets.

Because additionality is sometimes in the eye of the beholder, the UN has created delays and confusion in the marketplace by allowing some projects to qualify under CDM, but rejecting other similar projects. The UN also changed some of its rules in the middle of commitment periods, leaving offset-project developers stuck with expensive projects that reduced carbon but had little or no economic value. Regulators are tackling this challenge in different ways in different markets, but one way to avoid such confusion is to eliminate additionality tests and focus solely on nominal reductions: Did the project measurably reduce carbon emissions, regardless of who paid for it or why it was done? If so, it qualifies.

Under this nominal approach, the assumption of how much carbon is likely to go into the atmosphere each year will be higher than when using the additionality approach, because the latter calculation factors in reductions that are likely to occur from such things as renewable energy mandates. If you begin with an assumption that emissions will be higher, then regulators will demand steeper reductions to achieve the same net result by a given date; however more strategies will be embraced and the accounting will be more transparent.

Perhaps the granddaddy of all offset debates is the one focused on forests. No one disputes that growing trees absorb and sequester carbon. Clearing land releases carbon as organic materials decay. Some experts have argued therefore that CDM credits should be given for "avoided deforestation," that is, paying landowners not to cut down trees that might otherwise have been turned into dining-room tables or office credenzas. The UN decided not to qualify those projects for carbon offset credits because in many developing countries there is little or no enforcement and the land is often cleared anyway by farmers or poachers. There is also the question of avoiding logging in one place, while the demand for wood simply "leaks" to another forest somewhere else.

Instead, the UN only gives credit for projects that replant forests or add more trees to existing ones, projects that clearly reduce carbon and would not have happened without the funding from selling carbon credits. Several advocates for the "avoided deforestation" credits have gone on the offensive, however, creating an alliance called Reduced Emissions from Deforestation and Degradation (REDD) in developing countries to build more transparent and credible carbon offset programs that are the result of buying up forests. Some wealthy nations see this as a way to pay poorer nations to cooperate with international climate change treaties and initiatives; rather than allowing offset credits from these projects, the rich nations simply pay off the poor ones. Despite progress toward more support for REDD at the UN climate meetings in Copenhagen in 2009, it is not a reliable product for companies that are seeking to offset their own emissions.

The REDD debate highlights a simple point, however: when buying carbon-offset credits, *caveat emptor.* Despite bureaucratic fumbling during the early days of carbon markets, the UN and regulated markets such as the one in the EU have clarified what counts and what doesn't. Be sure to use authorized verification firms from which to get assurances about the validity of carbon credits your company buys (see the Resource Guide for companies and nonprofit organizations that can help with this task).

That leads to the final point about offsets. The market is flooded with carbon credits that were created to meet demand in the voluntary market and are not part of any regulated market. Many companies, such as Netjets, wanted to get ahead of regulation in order to meet customer demand, as well as to gain valuable experience in cracking the Carbon Code at very low cost. Voluntary projects may indeed have created real carbon reductions, but buyers must be very careful that their own credibility isn't damaged by purchasing credits—and bragging about doing things on a voluntary basis ahead of regulations—that may turn out to have little real value.

The two safest ways to ensure quality on the voluntary carbon offset market are to buy through a trusted exchange, such as the Chicago Climate Exchange, that imposes its own rules and verifications, or to apply the smell test as Governor Schwarzenegger did on the day of our Netjets meeting. If you buy offset credits from a project that you can't understand, the chances are that no one else will understand—or value—them either. Conversely, if the project clearly reduces carbon emissions to some degree, it is likely to make sense to your customers, who are the reason you bought the credits in the first place.

For example, Global Climate Strategies (www.globalclimat-estrategies.com) came up with a creative carbon offset project under CMD rules. The company bought thousands of compact fluorescent light bulbs and gave them to municipal buildings in Mexico at no cost. The project worked for CDM because it took place in a developing country whose cities were unlikely to incur the upfront costs of changing existing light bulbs all at once. Because government buildings could be monitored and the actual carbon reductions measured, CDM credits were issued for the project. It clearly passed the smell test, too.

Seeing the appetite for voluntary projects in the United States, Global Climate Strategies repeated the project north of the border, swapping bulbs for schools and other municipal buildings in communities that were struggling financially and would not likely have paid to change their lights all at once. Again, the carbon reductions were easy to measure and Global Climate Strategies created offset credits anyone could understand. The projects on both sides of the border had the added benefit of poorer communities saving money on future electric bills, something that everyone could easily understand and appreciate, especially when the company that buys the resulting carbon credits wants to brag about its good deeds.

Leasing the Sky Option 3: Buy Insurance

"The fines aren't that expensive," one utility executive told me confidentially, referring to the cost of noncompliance in a certain carbon regulatory scheme. "I mean, we're doing anything to cut greenhouse gases that has a one-year payback, but otherwise we'll just pay the fines. It's cheaper than changing anything else or buying those offsets."

It may not be good for PR purposes, but certainly the "pay the fines" approach is one carbon management strategy that acts as a kind of insurance—if all else fails, you can buy your way out. Assuming the regulators use the fines to fund other carbon reductions, you may actually have supported the overall goals of the program. Regulators are effectively taking away this option, however, by mandating that fines be paid but that doing so will not relieve the installation from surrendering the appropriate number of allowances for the relevant compliance period, sort of like paying fines to the IRS but still having to pay the taxes.

There are other forms of "insurance" that may be cheaper than fines and come with less stress to shareholders and consumers. "Banking" is the strategy most likely to cost the least, especially during the first few commitment periods under any regulatory scheme. To "bank" allowances, the installation reduces more than mandated, saving the resulting credits to use for its own future compliance (rather than selling the credits to another installation). When allowance auctions are held or other installations are selling excess credits, you may want to gamble that the price offered at the time is less than the price that is likely to prevail in future compliance periods, and buy credits in excess of current needs in order to bank them for the future. Finally, if allowed by regulators in your region, you might buy an excess of offsets from verified projects and use them later (or sell them at a profit) when the price of carbon rises.

Banking makes the most sense early in any carbon regulation. In the first few years of regulation in Europe, for example, regulators were liberal with caps on emissions and requirements on installations, so not surprisingly the price of carbon on open markets fell as demand remained low. Smart investors bought credits at a few euros per ton and held them for future years, knowing that regulators would tighten the caps and the cost of compliance would increase, making the credits worth much more. Indeed, the EU trading system saw credits rise to over 50 euros at one point, a tidy profit for anyone who had bought them early on.

The logic of this approach becomes clear when examining the McKinsey Curve. Many emissions reductions can be achieved with projects that pay for themselves, so companies won't be in the market for allowances or offsets. When that low-hanging fruit has been harvested, real reductions cost more as factories upgrade machines or install carbon-capture technology. Risk managers will compare the cost of those improvements against the cost of buying carbon on the open market, causing carbon credit values to rise. Banking today—at a good price—is a smart investment in the future.

Another "insurance" may be found in creating and/or trading Renewable Energy Credits (RECs, or Green Tags) or energy-efficiency credits (called White Tags). Most states (and some countries) have mandates on utilities to produce a certain percentage of electricity from clean renewable sources such as solar or wind power. In California, for example, utilities must secure 20 percent of their energy from renewables by 2010 and a third by 2020. These "renewable portfolio standards" (RPS) have resulted in a market for credits that result from clean energy projects. (See Appendix D for information on all state RPS programs.)

A green tag represents one megawatt-hour of electricity generated from a qualifying renewable energy source. To meet their obligations, utilities can generate their own renewable energy, buy renewable energy from other generators, or buy green tags so that renewable energy is created (and contributes to the RPS mandate) somewhere else. The green tags add revenue to projects and help defer some of the cost premium for things such as solar as compared to coal-fired power. Although a green tag clearly represents a reduction of carbon emissions, most regulated systems don't allow them to be used as carbon credits because of the additionality issue (the clean energy would have been produced in response to the RPS with or without added revenue from a carbon credit), but smart businesses may want to get involved with green tags anyway for two reasons.

First, generating renewable energy for your installation will reduce your own carbon footprint and therefore contribute to your obligation under any regulatory system. Because of the additionality issue, you may not be able to take any excess credits from your solar panels and sell them to someone else who needs a carbon credit, but you can sell the green tags to a utility that needs RPS credits, then use the proceeds to buy any additional carbon credits you need.

Second, for the same reason that carbon credits today are likely to be worth more in future years, green tags purchased or created today are likely to be worth more later, since utilities hit RPS deadlines and may fall short of goals, they face stiff fines and may be willing to pay more for green tags in your inventory than you originally paid. Again, this arbitrage is good for a company's bottom line. Proceeds can help offset the cost of carbon compliance in the future as the price of carbon escalates.

States such as Connecticut have created a similar market for energy efficiency credits—white tags—by setting mandates for energy efficiency improvements over time and forcing companies to prove they have either become more efficient or paid someone else in the state to do so. This idea is gaining traction in other jurisdictions as a policy strategy for reducing emissions of all kinds, so consider this another potential hedging strategy if such programs come to the places where your business operates.

Finally, actual insurance products can be purchased to mitigate risk from the impact of climate change, both physical and financial. Because insurance is purely a cost that reduces a company's bottom-line performance, it should be used only as a last resort. By cracking the Carbon Code—measuring, reducing, and managing your carbon footprint by using the tools in this book— insurance should not be necessary under most circumstances. That said, if you buy risk insurance for future carbon liabilities, try to lock in a premium for multiple years, because the cost of carbon will only increase over time.

Compare Your Business: Carbon Management Winners and Losers

Some have advocated placing a simple tax on carbon emissions as opposed to the complexity of a carbon market. In recent years, Wall Street market manipulation scandals and the failure of products such as sub-prime mortgage-backed derivative securities have tarnished the idea of a competitive market to achieve policy goals. Taxes, at least for the foreseeable future, are not politically feasible and don't assure policy results. For example, a tax on gasoline would probably need to be several dollars per gallon to motivate consumers to change consumption habits enough to reduce carbon emissions 10 or 20 percent over the next decade. Moreover, taxes stifle innovation; they are paid grudgingly and no one is motivated to find a lower-cost method of achieving the same policy goal. Finally, without a cap on emissions, which does exist in the cap-and-trade marketplace, there is no assurance that the policy goals will be achieved.

Considering these points, both businesses and political leaders have favored the market approach, and, given its track record of success in reducing other pollutants over time, it is likely to remain the policy option of choice in the United States as regulations evolve in states and ultimately at the federal level. Moreover, carbon markets have already gone global and will soon be linked. These markets and the products that serve them, such as offsets, will soon connect economic interests in the forests of Brazil with energy producers in California, driving costs even lower as the market, innovation, and competition expands. The total value of these efforts is growing exponentially, even ahead of a coordinated global system of regulations. In 2007, regulated market trades were valued at around $64 billion. Even the voluntary market that year topped $300 million, more than three times the market value of the previous year.

It's also likely that markets will grow faster in the next five years as the U.S. and global markets follow the course being set by California (and its partners in the Western Climate Initiative, as described in Appendix C), setting rules that allow an installation to meet up to half its obligations from offsets and other creative carbon management tools traded on the open market. Keep an eye on the development of those rules over future commitment periods at www.westernclimateinitiative.org. As Ben Franklin said, we all belong to one of three classes: those that are immovable, those that are movable, and those that move. Nothing could be more true in terms of managing carbon.

To underscore the point that innovation comes from capping emissions and allowing businesses to find the most cost-effective means of compliance, following are several examples of both winners and losers in the race to reduce carbon footprints.

Winners: Those Who Managed Their Carbon Footprints

Sun Microsystems (www.sun.com) found numerous ways to shrink its carbon footprint, and then even more clever ways to manage it. The software giant cut overall Scope 1 and 2 emissions by about four percent in the second year after it began measuring, which may not seem like much, but a steady four percent per year decline will keep the company well ahead of regulators. Sun also cut energy use by more than 50 million BTUs—adding money to the bottom line—with measures such as HVAC upgrades, lighting retrofits, building "tune-ups,"and installing variable speed drives on motors. Sun then focused on two parts of its footprint for management strategies, business travel and air freight shipping of its products. From 2007 to 2008, Sun was able to cut business travel two percent—again, not a big number, but impressive considering that business-as-usual would have seen that figure rise by double digits. The company also boasts that some 3,000 employees in the United States signed up for mass transit programs to cover their daily commutes. Finally, in FY2009, Sun addressed the largest, most obvious, and measurable source of carbon in its supply chain: air shipments. The company reduced the weight of products and improved logistics so that products travel shorter routes from manufacturing to end-users. The result? Sun cut emissions from that source by a third in one year.

As companies look to carbon markets for hedging strategies, the markets themselves will become very profitable. Climex (www.climex.com) provides an online trading platform for carbon credits of all kinds in Europe and will soon be expanding to the United States The new "stock exchange" will give risk managers options when they seek the lowest cost ton of carbon, offset, or seek to hedge with derivatives.

Companies that help clients manage carbon liabilities with strategies and offset products, along with companies that keep these markets trustworthy, will do very well in coming years. Two examples are Camco (www.camcoglobal.com), a strategy and offset product company, and APX (www.apx.com), which acts as a clearinghouse for buyers/sellers of these products, ensuring proper recording and clearing of transactions so that money changes hands properly and carbon credits are "retired" (used only once for compliance with regulatory schemes).

Losers: Those Who Failed to Manage Their Carbon Footprints

The obvious losers in this category are energy companies that can't do much to reduce their carbon footprints and don't have many cost-effective strategies to deal with such a large shoe size. A stark example exists in California, for example, where the Los Angeles Department of Water and Power (LADWP) relies on long-term contracts for coal-fired generation of more than a third of its power, while other large utilities in the state have already switched to cleaner sources such as natural gas, nuclear, and hydro. LADWP will be forced to buy allowances or offsets for its liability while the other utilities may have excess credits to sell because of advance carbon planning. Ameren (www.ameren. com), Reliant (www.reliant.com), and Mirant (www.mirant.com) are other examples of mostly coal-fired generators that operate in largely unregulated and highly competitive markets, giving them few ways to pass along carbon costs (as utilities in highly regulated regions can do) or to pay for hedging strategies (also very costly when the carbon footprint is so enormous).

A less obvious loser in this category is a company such as WM Barr (www.wmbarr.com), whose products will be impacted by both carbon and general air pollution concerns. Like the utilities that rely on coal-fired generation, there isn't much this company can do, dependent as it is for revenues on products like paints, thinners, and industrial solvents that have a high content of volatile organic compounds (VOCs) not easily replaced by other constituents. In California, which usually precedes national and international regulation, high-VOC-content products will be reduced or eliminated over time, starting in 2012, and will carry a much higher price because of inherent and unmanageable costs of carbon and toxins.

A World Bank study depicts nations and regions (figure 5.1) that can't manage their carbon footprints and will become carbon "losers." "Impact vulnerability" refers to climate change hazards, such as increased storms, droughts, floods, and sea-level rise.

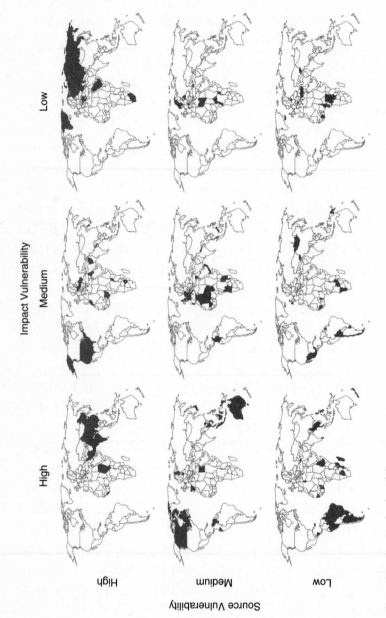

Figure 5.1 Regional vulnerability assessments

"Source vulnerability" refers to a region's access to fossil fuels and the potential size of short-term economic impacts when carbon has a global price. Source vulnerability makes countries less likely to commit to new carbon regulation/pricing, while impact vulnerability makes countries more likely to commit to carbon regulation. Companies with economic ties to source vulnerability are less likely to deal with carbon costs and present greater future risk. Based on the World Bank's assessment, the best places to invest—in carbon terms—are likely to be those with some combination of low impact vulnerability and high source vulnerability.

In Conclusion

Managing your carbon footprint requires the same ingenuity as cutting the carbon in the first place. As Fred Krupp and C. Boyden Gray demonstrated several decades ago, even unlikely allies can find common ground and solve complex problems. Because carbon emissions are a waste product—and no company wants to be inefficient—innovation is not a political issue, and managing a carbon footprint provides ways to create new, profitable products and services.

If you have cracked the Carbon Code up to this point you have the right to feel proud—you know more than 99 percent of investors and managers on the planet—but you're not done yet. How will evolving rules and markets change the way a company is positioned on the carbon scale? Will a company that successfully took the first steps have the resilience to remain ahead of the pack? The only way to know for sure if your strategy is a long- or short-term bet is to estimate your "carbon resilience."

Sources

Bayon, Ricardo, Amanda Hawn, and Katherine Hamilton. *Voluntary Carbon Markets* (London: Earthscan, 2009).

Brohe, Arnaud, Nick Ere, and Nicholas Howarth. *Carbon Markets: An International Business Guide* (London: Earthscan, 2009).

"C. Boyden Gray," Wikipedia, http://en.wikipedia.org/wiki/C._Boyden_Gray accessed October 1, 2009.

"Carbon Winners and Losers," *Forbes*, October 6, 2009.

"Climate Change Industry Aims to Be More Than a Silver Lining to Economic Clouds; Lloyd's Urges Insurers To Take Climate Change Seriously or Risk Being Swept Away," Lloyds of London, June 5, 2006.

Climate Winners and Losers, Energy Policy Information Center, November 3, 2009.

Buys, Piet, Uwe Deichmann, Craig Meisner, Thao Ton That, and David Wheeler, *Country stakes in climate change negotiations: two dimensions of vulnerability*, *Climate Policy*, 9, 288–305, 2009.

Ensuring Offset Quality: Design and Implementation Criteria for a High-Quality Offset Program, Three Regions Offset Working Group, May 2010.

"Fred Krupp, President, Environmental Defense Fund," biography accessed October 1, 2009 at http://www.edf.org/page.cfm?tagID=870.

Hoffman, Andrew J. *Carbon Strategies: How Leading Companies Are Reducing Their Climate Change Footprint* (Ann Arbor: University of Michigan Press, 2007).

"Let's Look Beyond the Haze," *Fast Company*, August 1, 2008.

Tamminen, Terry. "Would You Like Carbon Insurance with that Latte?" *Fast Company*, November 12, 2009.

Tamminen, Terry, Sasha Abelson, and Kristina Haddad. *Climate Change Handbook*. (Santa Monica: Seventh Generation Advisors Press, 2009).

"The Political History of Cap-and-Trade," *Smithsonian Magazine*, August 2009.

Sun Microsystems 2009 Corporate Social Responsibility Report, Sun Microsystems, 2009.

"The WCI Cap-and-Trade Program," http://www.westernclimateinitiative.org/the-wci-cap-and-trade-program, accessed December 28, 2009.

CHAPTER 6

Cracking the Carbon Code Step Five: Estimate Carbon Resilience

> People would say to us, 'You really don't have any skin in the game.' No one really thought about what it would do to our supply chain.
>
> —Brad Figel, Nike's director of government affairs, responding to comments that Nike shouldn't worry about climate change impacts

The U.S. Chamber of Commerce. Even without knowing that it is almost a century old and is regarded as the world's most powerful nonprofit lobbyist, "The Chamber" sounds like an inexorable force such as Darth Vader, the Roman Legions, or gravity. But knowing these things, knowing that it claims three million members, you know that when it speaks, people listen. Especially people in elected office. On the subject of carbon, the chamber reached back a century for its policy approach.

"The Chamber wants a Scopes monkey trial of the twenty-first century," said William Kovacs, the chamber's senior vice president for environment, technology, and regulatory affairs, describing a trial complete with witnesses, cross-examinations, and a judge who would rule, essentially, on whether humans are warming the planet to dangerous effect. "It would be Evolution versus Creationism. It would be the science of climate change on trial."

There are few membership organizations whose members are literally afraid of them, unwilling to break ranks regardless of how far afield some of its positions may be from those taken by individual members. For decades, disagreements among chamber stalwarts never broke out into the open, as dissenters feared retribution. But no force could prevent the dam from bursting once the first cracks appeared, over the topic of carbon.

Even when Duke Energy CEO Jim Rogers—the same CEO who sat with me and presidential candidate Obama in 2008 and agreed to work on energy efficiency and reducing carbon as a business necessity, not a tree-hugging charity—refused to renew membership in the National Association of Manufacturers, a baby brother trade group to the chamber that had also taken a stand against any kind of carbon regulation, the trouble didn't spill into the chamber. In fact, when the chamber's Kovacs called for a holy war on carbon in September of 2009, no one had yet dared to challenge Big Brother.

Another CEO from the Obama meeting that summer of 2008 was Peter Darbee of the California-based utility PG&E. Darbee had heard the chamber's position and had a Luke Skywalker moment. He could remain silent no longer. PG&E would challenge the mother-of-all-lobbyists and damn the torpedoes.

"We find it dismaying that the chamber neglects the indisputable fact that a decisive majority of experts have said the data on global warming are compelling and point to a threat that cannot be ignored," wrote Darbee in his company's letter of resignation from the lobbying behemoth. "In our opinion, an intellectually honest argument over the best policy response to the challenges of climate change is one thing; disingenuous attempts to diminish or distort the reality of these challenges are quite another."

Emboldened by Darbee, the carbon version of the Rebel Alliance took shape. Within weeks, Exelon, PNM Resources, Nike, Apple, Johnson & Johnson, and other influential members either resigned or called for the chamber to change its position. "The carbon-based free lunch is over," said Exelon CEO John W. Rowe. "Breakthroughs on climate change and improving our society's energy efficiency are within reach."

The Future Defined: Finding a Company's Carbon Resilience Ranking

The fracture between businesses of the old and new econo-mies has not been so clear since the evolution from horsepower to mechanized transport, or from gas lamps to electric light-ing. The dying old economy—represented by trade associations rooted in century-old thinking—is doing all it can to protect business-as-usual, an apple cart that is being rapidly tipped over by progressive, profitable businesses that have cracked the Carbon Code.

But after measuring, reducing, and managing a carbon foot-print, the way to determine if a company will be able to succeed in the new low-carbon economy of the future is to measure its ability to *continue* evolving. Monetizing efficiency and a few early action carbon credits won't make that change alone, but constant improvement and adaptation will. The final step in cracking the Carbon Code, therefore, is to evaluate if the long-term prospects are bright or dim based on three key factors: Carbon Financial Resilience, Hidden Carbon, and Industry Benchmarking.

Because so many of these factors are subjective, the final "score" won't be a number, but, as shown in figure 6.1, more like a place-ment relative to competitors and markets in general. Using the three key factors described in this chapter will help you place your company within the graph in figure 6.1.

Taken together, the three metrics in figure 6.1 give a business its Carbon Resilience Ranking, which can help to predict its car-bon, and financial, future.

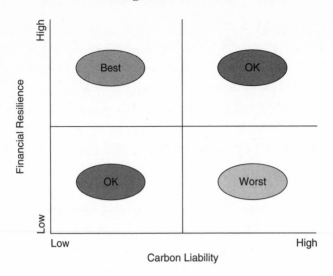

Figure 6.1   Finding the Carbon Resilience Ranking of a company

1   Carbon Financial Resilience: Ten Questions for Measuring Carbon Financial Resilience

There's an old joke about a guy who jumps off the top of the Empire State Building. As he passes the fiftieth floor on his way to inevitable doom, he is heard to mutter, "So far, so good."

Like the hapless jumper, carbon resilience is not just a matter of how a company might benefit or be challenged by a price on carbon today or in the near future, but of how the health of the business will be affected in the long term. Recognizing that any transition requires some changes, from retooling to investments in clean energy infrastructure, there are ten questions to ask to evaluate a company's financial resilience to oncoming carbon costs. Financial resilience is a measure of a company's cash on hand and annual cash flow plus the value of its various assets. Simply stated, how prepared is the company to deal with a new, unexpected expense, in this case the price on carbon, on its P&L or balance sheet?

There are ten questions that can be asked to get enough information to make an informed estimate of financial resilience to carbon costs and to place the company higher or lower on the Y-axis (financial resilience) in the Carbon Resilience Ranking graph. Remember that many carbon investments become profit centers—energy efficiency or renewable energy costs will be repaid with savings over time, but will have upfront costs that could impact a company's health in the near term. How able is a company to remain profitable if costs rise unexpectedly?

When evaluating a company's financial health, one basic rule generally applies: cash is king. That's also true for estimating a company's carbon financial resilience. Start by examining the profit and loss (P&L) statement, which describes how much net cash the business is generating. Headroom in net cash provides funds to improve energy efficiency or to replace fossil fuels with renewables. It also cushions the impact of any sudden new expense item, such as a carbon tax or higher fuel prices.

The source of revenues is another critical piece of information, because a P&L may show great cash flow, but if the revenues are coming largely from carbon-exposed sources, it could reveal less resilience than at first glance. If you are your company's environmental health and safety officer, or are assigned to evaluate the company's carbon resilience, here are key places to examine within the P&L, preferably over several years, to find signs of financial, and therefore carbon, resilience:

1. *Are the earnings before interest and taxes (EBIT) consistently strong?* Operating income is the key, including depreciation and amortization of assets that will need to be replaced over time (especially considering that equipment upgrades may be needed for energy efficiency or lower carbon manufacturing). It is equally important to see that the cost of goods sold, expressed as a percentage of sales revenues, tracks from year to year. If not, there may be the appearance of higher net revenues in a period of a few years that is unsustainable over the long term.

2. *Is the income real?* Look for excessive dependence on unrealized income to make the P&L look better than it actually is. Some years ago, Xerox sold copiers with multi-year maintenance contracts. To boost earnings in the short term, Xerox recognized almost all of the revenue in the first year, even

though maintenance expenses would be incurred in future years. While not illegal, Xerox essentially inflated net cash in the short term, but knew that earnings would decline when maintenance expenses kicked in and no revenues appeared on the income line to cover them. In a similar example, Waste Management Inc. (WMI) changed depreciation schedules for trucks and dumpsters to almost twice the industry standard, which made near-term profits soar, but of course those assets had to be replaced, incurring costs in later years when the company would still be depreciating the old fleet. A dumpster that lasts 20 years should have made someone suspicious. The scandal brought down the company at the time, but a sharp eye would have found the changes in depreciation in the P&L footnotes and raised a red flag. On that note, the footnotes of annual reports and financial statements hold many clues: depreciation choices; revenue recognition choices; dates when commitments were made to certain kinds of technologies or when upgrades are expected. All of these things could change the P&L in the future and should be factored into financial resilience estimates.

3. *Are capital expenses reasonable?* Harder to spot, another accounting trick involves amortizing ordinary business expenses as if they were durable goods or other capital investments, because it defers the true cost to future years (making the current year's costs seem lower and therefore net profit higher). Of course those ordinary business expenses will be incurred again, making net profits lower in future years.

4. *What line-item costs in the P&L represent 75 percent of total costs?* These are often only a few items, but they help to really understand the business. If any of those items are carbon heavy, their cost is likely to increase significantly over time. In one example, a shipping firm's direct costs totaled $13.5 million, of which fuel cost $8.1 million, 60 percent of the direct costs. Knowing that fossil fuel is such a large part of the company's cost structure should be a warning to management that profits might fall as a price on carbon is added. However, there could also be carbon benefits hidden in these

costs. For example, PG&E operates clean natural gas-fired power plants, which emit far less carbon than coal- or oil-fueled generators. As such, even though the company spends a lot on fuel, knowing that it is a cleaner fuel to begin with is a signal that there may be early action carbon credits or other benefits when a competitor's costs go up and PG&E's go down, in both cases because of the relative carbon content of their respective fuels. Recall the problem facing LADWP described in chapter 5, which may soon be buying such credits from PG&E, creating a new cost for the former and a new profit for the latter that may not be obvious today unless you are looking for each company's carbon. It is equally important to avoid overestimating the potential costs of a price on carbon. Several studies provide a range of likely added costs that may be useful in this analysis, assuming $40 a ton for carbon by 2020 in California. Energy costs there are typically among the nation's highest, so these figures represent the worst likely scenario in the U.S. to calculate the potential added cost of carbon by fuel type:

- 0.7 cents per kWh for electricity (the California Renewable Portfolio standard may add an average of 1.1 cents per kHh by then, a figure which will vary in each state that has an RPS);
- 15 cents per therm for natural gas;
- 35 cents per gallon for transportation fuel.

5. *Is most of the company's revenue from one core competency that could change under carbon regulation?* For example, as highlighted in chapter 3, the Australian company CHEP rents wooden shipping pallets, but because of carbon policies that penalize the cutting down of forests, plastic pallets are rapidly replacing the old-school models. Plastic pallets are a third lighter, so transportation costs are lower, which will be rewarded more when carbon is fully priced. Another example is Waste Management (WMI) in the 1990s. In addition to the accounting fraud mentioned previously, WMI bought non-core businesses in an effort to expand and increase revenues.

It was quickly clear that WMI might be good at taking out the trash, but knew little about the new businesses it now owned. Not surprisingly, this resulted in losses which pressured the C-suite to cook the books with those bogus depreciation figures. Companies whose revenues depend heavily on new acquisitions, which may not be core to the business, may experience a loss of financial resilience in the future.

6. *Can the business raise prices to match new costs?* In the 1980s, I managed a ranch that grew corn. It cost $2 per bushel to grow, but at harvest time we could only sell it for $1.80 because of the commodity markets. In most businesses, when the cost of goods sold goes up, so do prices for the finished products. Farming is one of those industries without that flexibility. Such inflexibility obviously impacts financial resilience.

7. *Do assets outweigh liabilities?* The P&L gives you a sense of financial resilience month-to-month and year-to-year, but what has the company amassed in terms of assets and liabilities that may help or hinder its ability to deal with new carbon realities in the future? The balance sheet is another Rosetta Stone in determining both financial and carbon resilience. The most obvious indicator of financial resilience on a balance sheet is the verification that the company's assets outweigh its liabilities, so that the owner's equity is a positive number. Look also at several years of balance sheets to verify that such equity has grown over time. The other significant asset is cash. A strong cash position can provide capital for reducing carbon and increasing efficiency. It's also the hardest asset on a balance sheet to obscure by the "art" of finance that might be behind other line items.

8. *Is the debt-to-equity ratio low?* Lower is better (less than two to one) for resilience in case investments (and possibly further debt) are needed to help de-carbonize the business.

9. *Are the assets themselves carbon-heavy?* In the earlier example about wooden shipping pallets, CHEP's balance sheet may list hundreds of millions of dollars in pallets that it owns, but if the price on carbon, and policies against deforestation, move the market toward plastic pallets, those assets will soon

be worth much less. By contrast, the plastic pallets owned by companies such as iGPS are probably undervalued on its balance sheet when those same carbon dynamics are applied.

10. *What is the company worth?* The balance sheet is often used by bankers to value a company that may be for sale or is the subject of a merger (and companies are always for sale at the right price). Valuation of a company may reveal hidden assets in terms of market value, but which are not necessarily good measures of financial resilience. For example, you can't convert an asset such as a building into solar panels that reduce carbon costs. In fact, heavy investments in real estate in regions that are served by coal-fired power plants may be a liability as carbon prices rise, even if in the near term the assets have a high market value. Similarly, recent purchases of durable goods that tie you to fossil fuels (oil-fired boilers, for example, or fleets of diesel trucks) may be signs of stuck-in-carbon thinking rather than assets that will retain value over time.

2   Hidden Carbon: The Five Signs of Hidden Carbon

Uncovering carbon that may not appear in a footprint analysis or on financial reports will help determine if early carbon success can be continued or will grind to a halt. A careful review of a company's assets may also reveal good news, hidden low-carbon products or infrastructure that can be monetized in a carbon-constrained world. A P&L or balance sheet may get healthier very quickly when carbon has a price if the company has hidden carbon assets to monetize.

The Five Signs of Hidden Carbon, which place the company to the left or the right on the X-axis of the Carbon Resilience Ranking graph, are:

1. *Did the company take action to reduce carbon ahead of regulations, and are there potential early action credits as a result that may add unexpected revenues? What baseline year did the company use?*

It will determine how many years of early action credits may be available now.

2. *Has the company upgraded basic equipment or installations in recent years?* In an energy-intensive business, look for signs that the company has not upgraded equipment for many years. Chances are this means carbon reductions can be achieved with energy efficiency retrofits that pay for themselves. Lower costs obviously improve the bottom line and financial resilience, but also reduce potential carbon costs. Of course, businesses that have already taken significant energy efficiency measures will be carbon ready, and any added cost of carbon will be easier to forecast, but the potential benefits to the net profit may be less dramatic.

3. *Does the company sell products that may contain hidden carbon from things you wouldn't normally associate with such emissions, such as water?* In California, for example, the pumping, moving, delivery, and treatment of water is responsible for the largest use of electricity—about 20 percent of all generation in the state. That translates into a third of the state's non–power plant natural gas use and about 100 million gallons of diesel burned every year, resulting in an estimated 44 million tons of carbon emissions annually. Products that use a lot of water will own a piece of that substantial carbon footprint. A hidden carbon asset might be found in products that conserve water—low flow bathroom fixtures, for example, or industrial processes that use less water such as those pioneered by Interface and Bentley Prince Street (see chapter 3).

4. *Is management carbon-ready?* Hidden carbon assets may also exist in the C-suite or boardroom. A corporate mindset that is preparing for a low-carbon future, instead of resisting it, can be a company's most valuable asset in terms of financial and carbon resilience. Consider asking these questions to find evidence of such preparation:

   • *Does the board have members with expertise in carbon regulation and markets?*

- *Does any member of the C-suite have a demonstrated competence in carbon markets or hedging strategies?*
- *Has the board or C-suite created alliances with key carbon experts, such as carbon offset developers, government regulatory design work groups, carbon traders, or partners in the same industry that operate in regions where carbon has already been regulated for many years, such as the EU?*

5. *Of which trade associations is the company a member?* Another simple tool for determining the executive mindset and carbon readiness can be found in the positions taken by the company in the trade organizations in which it maintains membership. Those companies that still defend the U.S. Chamber's witch-trial position on carbon, for example, can hardly be considered ready for the low-carbon future. Those that have publicly broken ranks may exhibit more foresight and therefore more carbon resilience in the future.

3   Benchmark against Industry Competitors: The Six Carbon Oracles

Given that all competitors in an industry will face the same basic challenge of decarbonizing, the real metric for Carbon Resilience may not be internal, but a measure against industry standards. As a former regulator, I can report that government tends to aim for the center. It wants to make life easy for the majority and to crack down on only the worst offenders. Carbon resilience will be no different: those companies that crack the Carbon Code and get ahead of regulations will be much better placed than those seen as lagging.

Several tools are available for this evaluation, which place companies to the left or right of the X-axis on the Carbon Resilience Ranking graph. There are dozens of nonprofits, analytics, and news services related to carbon, but the Six Carbon Oracles are all that a smart manager or investor will need. They are:

1. *The Carbon Disclosure Project.* CDP (www.cdproject.net) is a nonprofit organization that maintains a database of companies' carbon assets, liabilities, and actions taken to reduce

carbon, their "disclosures." CDP encourages institutional investors to make carbon a key metric in making investment decisions using this information. Over 2,000 companies now report to CDP, providing two valuable resources to managers. First, the data is assembled and made publicly available so that cumbersome forensic research in corporate records, annual reports, and other data isn't necessary to get the most relevant carbon information. Second, CDP allows a company to compare itself to others in the same industry, and all companies can be compared to carbon regulation locally, nationally, or internationally. CDP assembles the data and provides carbon readiness scores, making quantitative analysis more accurate and actionable.

2. *Bloomberg New Carbon Finance* (http://carbon.newenergy finance.com) is a for-profit information service (so, unlike CDP, it charges for most data) that provides news that may affect carbon resilience, industry indices for such things as renewable energy stocks, analysis of carbon offset projects, and rankings of companies in terms of carbon assets and liabilities.

3. *The Climate Change Business Journal* (www.climatechange business.com) offers relevant carbon news, but also provides analysis of ten key segments of the carbon industry itself, including:

- Climate change consulting
- Solar energy and wind power
- Carbon trading
- Carbon capture and storage
- Bioenergy, biomass and biofuels
- Energy efficiency and demand response
- Consulting and engineering
- Green building
- Renewable energy consulting
- Climate change adaptation

Studying these industries, and their clients, can provide added valuable carbon intelligence for evaluating your company's carbon resilience.

4. *CERES* (www.ceres.org) is another nonprofit that helps define sustainability, including the contribution of carbon, for institutional investors and companies alike. Members adopt various sustainability principles, including significant disclosure of carbon assets and liabilities. CERES also conducts valuable research and holds conferences that give companies and investors useful information ahead of regulation or the imposition of new costs.

5. *MetaVu* (www.metavu.com) is a consulting firm that has developed a novel "spider web" graph to rank a company relative to objective sustainability and carbon efficiency standards against competitors, and against an industry. Managers and investors can see how carbon-resilient a company may be, but also evaluate the strengths of the carbon assets and just how risky the carbon liabilities really are.

6. *Enviance* (www.enviance.com) is a web-based analytics firm that provides companies with tools to measure dynamic changes to a wide variety of environmental metrics, including carbon. Enviance products are tailored to every level of corporate management, providing actionable data that can help a company get (and stay) ahead of regulations and discover hidden carbon liabilities or assets.

Compare Your Business: Carbon Resilience
Winners and Losers

Unlike other aspects of cracking the Carbon Code, understanding or improving a company's carbon resilience is as much art as it is science, especially in the years leading up to a more well-defined and regulated carbon market. In addition to the metrics presented in this chapter, it will help evaluate your company by looking at examples of other companies with high or low carbon resilience.

Winners: Those with High Carbon Resilience Rankings

One of the more pleasant duties of a Secretary of the California Environmental Protection Agency is handing out recognition for groundbreaking eco-accomplishments and citizens. In 2004, I was asked to visit Toyota's North American Parts Center in Ontario, California, a 734,000-square-foot auto parts distribution center. Throughout the tour, I saw the word *kaizen* printed on walls, doors, ceilings, and windows—a Japanese term that expresses the idea that no matter how good something is, you can always improve it. I also saw little signs that told me which employees had thought of the sustainability ideas (many of them carbon-reducing) that together had resulted in the facility receiving the 2004 WRAP Award (Waste Reduction Awards Program). Ideas that saved resources, including energy and money, included the creation of returnable shipping boxes that saved some 600 tons of wood and over 80 tons of cardboard. Lighter materials also meant less carbon emissions from fuel use during shipping. The facility diverted 654 tons of waste from landfills, saving about $1.4 million annually in direct costs. This *kaizen* approach is a great sign that Toyota (www.toyota.com) has taken steps to lower carbon liabilities and has also made itself more carbon resilient with constant improvement.

You wouldn't think you could teach an old dog new tricks, but 26-billion-dollar, 100-year-old Alcoa (www.alcoa.com) has aggressively pursued sustainability goals for the past generation. The company recognized that not all greenhouse gases are created equal, so while it made efficiency improvements and took other carbon-busting steps across the board, it focused on the gases that were creating the most disproportionate carbon footprint. Alcoa found it could reduce perfluorocarbons (PFCs) by changing the electrolysis process in its smelting operations, and PFCs are 7,400 times more potent heat-trapping gases than CO_2. Alcoa also found that recycled aluminum creates only 5 percent of the carbon footprint that metals do from virgin ore, so it committed to getting 50 percent of the metals for new products from recycled materials by 2020. That lawn chair made with Alcoa aluminum will have a much lower carbon content than the competitor's, made from a source that didn't recycle. Think too about products that are equal in every respect, except that one was made where electricity comes from coal-fired power plants and the other from cleaner energy sources such as hydro or natural gas. It doesn't take a carbon scientist to tell you which one saves more money and has the lower carbon footprint, or which company is the more carbon-resilient.

Palm Plastics (http://palmplastics.com) in Morenci, Michigan, sits outside the rusting car capital of America, Detroit, and the company's fortunes have always been inextricably connected to the auto industry. In 2008, I toured Palm's main manufacturing center, a few yards from the border of Michigan and Ohio, two states that have lost much of their once-proud industrial productivity. A sign on a small bridge over a stream that separates the states boasts that you can stand at its apex and straddle both states simultaneously. Inside the familiar tilt-up walls of the factory was a small meeting room festooned with products once made there— car bumpers, door panels, knobs, and dashboards—hundreds of different molded plastic components that are part of the typical American car. But because of the economic downturn in the industry, Palm no longer makes a single one of those parts, testimony to the fact that their primary customers were not carbon resilient and had been almost put out of business by foreign competitors. In the corner of the meeting room stood the one product that Palm actually still does manufacture—an iGPS shipping pallet (as described in chapter 3). The carbon-reducing pallet was being built on six assembly lines employing hundreds of workers, who otherwise would have joined their counterparts in the unemployment lines. The financial resilience of Palm depended entirely on the carbon resilience of iGPS, and both came out winners.

Losers: Those with Low Carbon Resilience Rankings

In April 2006, Governor Schwarzenegger did his Oprah imitation for hundreds of onlookers in the San Francisco City Hall. Mic in hand and roaming the stage like a rock star on a concert night, Schwarzenegger moderated a panel discussion on our proposed Climate Action Plan. Discussing his ideas for a carbon market and other limits on greenhouse gases were former USEPA administrator Bill Reilly, state assembly member Fran Pavley, and Tom Tietz, the executive director of the California Nevada Cement Association. Tietz argued vehemently that cement companies would move out of state if California imposed a cost on carbon. Many businesses made those claims, but most were hollow. In the case of cement, he had a point. Equipment can easily be moved across state lines, or into Mexico, and set up elsewhere. That's why the cement industry now has a major target on its collective back as regulators try to squeeze carbon out of the construction industry worldwide. Standards are being set to define "low-carbon" cement (product made in kilns using clean fuels or blending supplemental materials, such as fly ash) and many jurisdictions are mandating its use, just as was done to set standards for efficient lighting. As a result, cement from China that is high-carbon, for example, won't be able to compete with products that have a verifiable lower carbon footprint. Mr. Tietz and his industry have fought these changes, but cement makers will have to evolve or perish. Cement is the "glue" that makes all components of concrete harden, so both industries will suffer until it becomes clear which providers are adopting the low-carbon products. Until then, keep your portfolio clear of all cement and concrete providers.

Losers can also be found within industries that are otherwise quite carbon resilient. CERES publishes the Climate Watch List (www.ceres.org), which parsed out the industry laggards of 2009:

- In electric power: Southern Company (www.southerncompany.com)
- In coal: Massey Energy (www.masseyenergyco.com) and Consol Energy (www.consolenergy.com)
- In the oil and gas sector: Ultra Petroleum (www.ultrapetroleum.com), Exxon Mobil (www.exxonmobil.com), Chevron (www.chevron.com), and Canadian Natural Resources (www.cnrl.com) especially because of its tar sands liabilities
- Automotive: GM (www.GM.com)
- Home builders: Standard Pacific (www.standardpacifichomes.com)

CERES also engineers shareholder resolutions that encourage carbon resilience in these companies, persuading institutional investors to vote with their pocketbooks, another factor for companies to consider as it pertains to their ability to keep investors happy.

Finally, in the fast-food industry, there is no greater head-in-the-sand carbon laggard than Burger King (www.bk.com). Not only does the chain rely on beef (remember the description in chapter 4 on the carbon shock coming to the meat industry?) and fossil-fueled energy (for cooking fuel, transportation fuel, and electricity for heavy-duty refrigerators and lighting), but they consistently score among the lowest in terms of taking action to measure and reduce their carbon footprint. Both the consulting firm ENDS Carbon (www.endscarbon.com) and the nonprofit climatecounts.org counted BK as an industry laggard, the latter giving them a score of 10 out of a possible 100 for failing to take any meaningful action to improve carbon resilience, and for actively opposing carbon laws and markets, including using its store signage to declare "Global Warming Is Baloney."

In Conclusion

You have now completed the short course in cracking the Carbon Code. There are a few more tips and a handy summary that follow, but you are now armed and ready for the new low-carbon economy, well ahead of more than 99 percent of investors, shareholders, managers, and government officials on Earth.

The U.S. Chamber of Commerce may be stuck in the last century, but smart investors and businesses are cracking the Carbon Code for themselves, rendering old-fashioned trade associations increasingly irrelevant. As Brad Figel implied in his response to critics of Nike's progressive policies on carbon, we all have skin in this game, and we all need to move our environment and economy into a more sustainable twenty-first century ASAP.

Sources

2003 Waste Reduction Awards Program (WRAP), California Integrated Waste Management Board, www.calrecycle.ca.gov/WRAP/, accessed January 6, 2010.

"Apple Quits Chamber of Commerce Over Climate Change," *Huffington Post*, October 5, 2009.

Are You Carbon Ready? Heidrick & Struggles International, Inc., 2009.

Berman, Karen, and Joe Knight.*Financial Intelligence for Entrepreneurs* (Boston: Harvard Business School Publishing, 2008).

"Brand Emissions Leaders and Laggards Identified," ENDS Carbon, October 29, 2009.

Breaking the Climate Deadlock: Technology for a Low Carbon Future, The Climate Group, 2009.

"Burger King Franchises Try to Sell Climate Change Denial," watchingthewatchers. org, June 9, 2009.

Carbon Disclosure Leadership Index 2008, Carbon Disclosure Project, www.cdproject. net, accessed January 4, 2010.

China's Clean Revolution, The Climate Group, 2009.

"Climate Bill Splits Exelon and U.S. Chamber," *New York Times*, September 29, 2009.

Climate Change Business Journal, January/February/March 2009.

"Company Scorecard: Burger King," climatecounts.org. accessed January 5, 2010.

"Duke Energy Quits the Right-Wing National Association of Manufacturers over Differences on Climate Policy," Think Progress, May 8, 2009.

"Firms Start to See Climate Change as Barrier to Profit," *Washington Post*, September 21, 2009.

Hoffman, Andrew J.*Carbon Strategies: How Leading Companies Are Reducing Their Climate Change Footprint* (Ann Arbor: University of Michigan Press, 2007).

"Irreconcilable Differences," Next 100, September 22, 2009.

Issues and Options for Benchmarking Industrial GHG Emissions, Stockholm Environment Institute, May 12, 2010.

Levitt, Steven D., and Stephen J..*Freakonomics: A Rogue Economist Explores the Hidden Side of Everything (P.S.)* (New York: Harper Perennial, 2009).

"Oregon Regulators Drop Support for Cement Plant Rule," Associated Press, September 5, 2009.

"Southern, Massey Energy and Chevron among Nine 'Climate Watch' Companies Targeted by Investors," CERES, February 18, 2009.

The Economic Impact of AB32 on California Small Businesses, The Brattle Group and Union of Concerned Scientists, December 2009.

"U.S. Chamber of Commerce Seeks Trial on Global Warming," *Los Angeles Times*, August 25, 2009.

CHAPTER 7

Conclusion and Quick-Start Guide

> The idea that anything is possible.... It's like hey, look there's the moon up there, let's take a walk on it, bring back a piece of it. That's the kind of America that I'm a fan of.
>
> —Bono, lead singer of the band U2

"Imagine it's 100 years ago," California Governor Arnold Schwarzenegger wrote in the London newspaper *The Sun* in April 2009.

> Your business in 1909 would have relied on technologies such as gas lamps, ice boxes, the telegraph and horse-drawn buggies. Within a decade, those were replaced by electric lights, refrigeration, telephones and automobiles. A century of prosperity followed. The industrial transformation of the twentieth century was built on fossil fuels that are rapidly running out. What is more, 100 years ago we didn't know any better—but have since learned that burning oil and coal

pollutes our air, causes asthma and lung cancer and drastically changes our climate. Economic prosperity in the twenty-first century—the Sustainable Century—will be defined by businesses built on clean, renewable, globally abundant resources made available to everyone.

Never mind that these insightful comments appeared under a photo of Schwarzenegger as the film character The Terminator, with half of his face blown away revealing a cyborg with a glowing red eyeball. He went on to point out something that is the real reason the low-carbon economy will "terminate" the fossil-fueled one faster than anyone can imagine today.

"Think about it," he continued. "Coal, oil and uranium are 'elite fuels,' controlled by a few and limited by Mother Nature. But all of us have unfettered access to the sun, wind, things that grow, moving water and other clean, inexhaustible, renewable sources of energy, so that's not just smarter, it's democratic. Businesses run on energy, so by democratizing our energy supply, we democratize our economy—and teach the world how to democratize theirs."

Unlimited energy supply, free from pollution. Economic freedoms unimaginable today, equal opportunity for billions of people in China, India, and even in the United States, who today are constrained by old technology, scarce and expensive resources, and the threat of disease and climate-change impacts. As more people understand these dynamics, the world won't need oracles of inconvenient truths to motivate change.

The purpose of this final chapter is to offer two valuable tools to keep you in front of this economic tidal wave. First are a few ideas about how to decipher changes to the Carbon Code over time to keep the skills you have gained from reading this book current and actionable. Second, we have become accustomed to complex devices and tools that come with a "quick-start guide," so whether you have read every chapter or have skimmed ahead, this chapter includes a convenient chart to remind you of key steps in cracking the Carbon Code and where to find details in the text as needed.

The Three Secrets of Staying on Top of the Carbon Code

Having cracked the Carbon Code by following the five steps presented thus far, here are the three tips for acting on your unique knowledge and for keeping on top of changes that will occur in future years with regulators and consumers.

1   *Appoint a Carbon Manager for Your Company*

Until a few years ago, most companies neither had nor had heard of a corporate EH&S officer (environmental health and safety), but today almost every successful enterprise has someone with those specific duties and title. A few years from now, no company will be without a carbon manager, not only because it is an area such as EH&S that requires specialized compliance knowledge, but because it will be a significant source of a company's revenue or cost structure.

There are very few areas of a business that will change as rapidly in the next few years as the world of carbon. Getting ahead of this trend will ensure that someone is specifically responsible to save the company money by decarbonizing and by complying with new carbon laws and regulations. A specific carbon officer will also compare the company to industry norms and keep your products competitive as carbon footprints become more important in the supply chain and to consumers.

2   *As the Company Carbon Manager, Go Back to Steps 2 and 3 Often*

Steps 2 and 3 are the heart of making your company more carbon resilient after cracking the Carbon Code: measure your carbon footprint often, and keep looking for ways to cut the carbon.

Measuring is cheap and, as the McKinsey Curve shows, reducing your carbon footprint can actually save money. As you get to Step 4, managing the remaining carbon footprint and paying for your emissions is the last thing any company wants to do, because it automatically incurs new cost. Become an expert in Steps 2 and 3 to make sure your carbon footprint doesn't include anything that should be inside another installation's fenceline, and once you are sure you know what your responsibility is, engage every employee and vendor in finding innovative ways to cut the carbon. *Kaizen*—constant improvement—will save money and make your company increasingly competitive as carbon regulations emerge and costs inevitably rise.

Similarly, consider hedging your future needs by creating or buying carbon credits ahead of need. The experience of the EU and others shows that carbon will never be cheaper than in the early years of regulation (or ahead of regulation). Buying credits that can be banked for compliance purposes in future years, or selling to those who need them, will pay big dividends over time.

3   Go West, Young Man

The old saying from America's expansion in the 1800s is true today in terms of looking westward for clues to how carbon regulation will develop nationally and how carbon markets will be created globally. California has always been a leader in environmental regulation and its congressional delegation has never been more powerful than in recent years.

As such, and because California was the first state to pass a carbon law, it is reasonable to predict that steps taken by the Golden State will be copied by other states and ultimately the federal government. Tailpipe emissions for vehicles were first promulgated in California and later adopted nationally by the Obama administration, and, grudgingly, by car makers. California's appliance efficiency standards, renewable energy programs, and its creation of the Western Climate Initiative for a carbon market that covers much of North America, will all lead to regulations and opportunities nationwide.

To stay on top of this California pebble in the carbon pond, watch these four key websites:

- For regulation and product standards: California's Global Warming Solutions Act (AB32) Implementation at http://www.arb.ca.gov/cc/cc.htm
- For carbon-market design and implementation: the Western Climate Initiative at www.westernclimateinitiative.org

- For international connection to U.S.-based carbon regulation and markets: International Carbon Action Partnership at www.icapcarbonaction.com.
- For context and insights on California and international carbon developments: Seventh Generation Advisors at www. seventhgenerationadvisors.org.

A Carbon Code Quick-Start Guide

If carbon is a fairly new topic to you, reading the five steps of cracking the Carbon Code may be enlightening but somewhat of a challenge to keep straight. The chart in Table 7.1 is a reminder of the basics and where to find the details in the main part of the text.

In Conclusion

In 2007 I was traveling with Governor Schwarzenegger on a policy and trade mission to Canada. A reporter asked what I thought of recently announced climate policies of Prime Minister Stephen Harper. Although I had helped several provinces develop California-style climate-action plans, which put them on a par with leading nations under the Kyoto Protocol, the Canadian federal government had aligned itself with U.S. President Bush at the time, essentially content to ignore both its global obligation or low-carbon opportunities. I said as much to the reporter, condemning the shortsightedness of both governments.

The trip included a quick stop in Ottawa to meet the prime minister before a final stop in Vancouver. Schwarzenegger's chief of staff got word before we left Toronto that "we look forward to exchanging views with the governor, but Mr. Tamminen is persona non grata." I was sent ahead to Vancouver and the governor met with Harper alone.

Although I wasn't trying to irk Harper with my candid comments, I was trying to make a point that has since proven true; that is, you can't solve the climate-change challenge or take advantage of economic opportunity by ignoring both.

Table 7.1 A carbon code quick start checklist

Carbon Code Step	Key Actions	Page
1. Time Your Carbon Tipping Point (three key questions tell you when to act)	1. When will my business or industry be regulated?	28
	2. When will my customers demand that I deal with my company's carbon footprint?	32
	3. When will the impacts of climate change affect the assets or business model of my company?	33
2. Build a Fence (three carbon metrics for determining your carbon footprint correctly)	1. Determine your carbon footprint.	43
	2. Use the right carbon yardstick.	47
	3. Record your carbon footprint with the right Registry.	51
3. Cut the Carbon (three rules of Carbon Gravity find lowest cost carbon busters)	1. Invest in energy efficiency.	65
	2. Switch to renewables.	68
	3. Look on the floor.	69
4. Manage What Can't Be Cut (three cost-effective ways to lease the sky)	1. Buy allowances.	81
	2. Buy offsets.	83
	3. Buy insurance.	89
5. Estimate Carbon Resilience (keep ahead of regulations and consumers)	1. Estimate carbon financial resilience.	102
	2. Discover hidden carbon.	107
	3. Benchmark against your industry.	109

The lesson for smart managers and businesses is to think like Schwarzenegger. There are certainly honest and valuable differences of opinion about the best way to decarbonize industry and move to the "sustainable century," as the governor called it. But there can no longer be any doubt that the time has come.

Having learned to crack the Carbon Code, you are now armed with the tools to take advantage of the low-carbon economy and keep your company from going the way of dinosaurs, the horse-and-buggy, and a few myopic politicians.

Now get started, and good luck.

Source

"How the Sun Can Change the Earth," *The Sun*, April 21, 2009.

RESOURCE GUIDE

The following are organizations and resources that can help you learn more about the topics covered in this book. They include consultants, nonprofits, and websites for organizations that have expertise in the evolving world of carbon regulations, including how to measure carbon footprints, reduce emissions, and miti- gate liability with carbon offsets and trading. Because the field is growing rapidly, any such list must be constantly updated.

One website that can help you to keep current with all of the other sources is www.TheCarbonCode.com, the "carbon base camp" created by myself and my team to give you a great head start in managing your carbon liabilities and assets. Other resources are organized in the following pages based on the primary form of information or service they provide.

Policy and Data-Tracking Sources

While there is no lack of data and advice to help a business to manage carbon, it is sometimes hard to separate information that is actionable from that which is just FYI or even merely rumor. The sources below have consistently provided a valuable context with the information they provide.

American Council for an Energy-Efficient Economy (www.aceee.org). A nonprofit organization dedicated to advanc- ing energy efficiency as a means of promoting economic prosper- ity, energy security, and environmental protection.

Carbon Disclosure Project (www.cdproject.net). An indepen- dent nonprofit organization holding the largest database of primary corporate climate change information in the world. Thousands of organizations from across the world's major economies measure and disclose their greenhouse gas emissions and climate change strategies through CDP.

Center for Clean Air Policy (www.ccap.org). The publications section of this site provides information on emissions trading and other issues related to climate change. The center, which was founded by a bipartisan group of state governors, focuses on market-based approaches to environmental problems.

Center for Climate Strategies (www.climatestrategies.us). CCS works with governors and other state leaders to develop statewide climate action plans with comprehensive policy solutions, broad bipartisan stakeholder support, and successful implementation. In addition, they provide specialized technical and policy assessments and planning support related to climate, energy, and economic issues.

Clean Tech Investor (www.cleantechinvestor.com). A publisher of finance, investment, and business information, focusing on the cleantech space.

Climate Counts (www.climatecounts.org). A collaborative effort to bring consumers and companies together in the fight against global climate change. Its website features the Climate Counts Company Scorecard to compare an enterprise to other companies in their sector.

Database of State Incentives for Renewables and Efficiency (www.dsireusa.org). DSIRE is a comprehensive source of information on utility, local, state, and federal incentives that promote renewable energy and energy efficiency. The database is an ongoing project of the North Carolina Solar Center and the Interstate Renewable Energy Council (IREC) funded by the U.S. Department of Energy.

Energy Foundation (www.ef.org). A partnership of major donors interested in solving the world's energy problems. Their mission is to advance energy efficiency and renewable energy, embracing new technologies that are essential components of a clean energy future.

Greener World Media (www.greenerworldmedia.com). Information, resources, and learning opportunities to help companies of all sizes and sectors integrate environmental responsibility into their operations in a manner that supports profitable business practices; includes Green Biz news (www.greenbiz.com).

Intergovernmental Panel on Climate Change (http://www. ipcc.ch/organization/organization.htm). The leading body for the assessment of climate change science, established by the United Nations Environment Programme (UNEP) and the World Meteorological Organization (WMO) to provide the world with a clear scientific view on the current state of climate change and its potential environmental and socioeconomic consequences.

Massachusetts Institute of Technology Joint Program on the Science and Policy of Global Change (http://globalchange.mit. edu/). An interdisciplinary program focused on independent policy analysis and research on global environmental change issues.

NOAA Climate Services (www.climate.gov/#climateWatch). A portal for a wide variety of climate data, products, and services for all types of users.

Pew Center for Global Climate Change (www.pewclimate. org). A nonprofit organization whose mission is to provide credible information and innovative solutions in the effort to address global climate change.

Point Carbon (www.pointcarbon.com). Provider of independent news, analysis, and consulting services for European and global energy and carbon markets. Provides professionals with market-moving information through monitoring fundamental information, key market players, and business and policy developments.

Progressive Investor (www.sustainablebusiness.com). A monthly, online green investing newsletter that guides people toward investments in companies leading the way to a green economy. Helps individuals and managers understand the trends and identify the leading green companies.

Seventh Generation Advisors (www.seventhgeneration advisors.org). Devises programs for numerous U.S. state governors, global institutions, investors, and companies on sustainability, climate change, and clean energy policies worldwide. Its website provides a comprehensive Carbon Policy Handbook, policy updates and forecasts, and detailed evaluations of state policies and programs. Author Terry Tamminen is the president of Seventh Generation Advisors.

State and Local Climate and Energy Program (www.epa.gov/statelocalclimate). This website brings together USEPA resources to serve as a one-stop shop for government officials seeking information on climate change and clean energy.

Union of Concerned Scientists (www.ucsusa.org). The leading science-based nonprofit which combines independent scientific research and citizen action to develop innovative, practical solutions and to secure responsible changes in government policy, corporate practices, and consumer choices. Their website contains excellent reports and data on the science of climate change, including information on impacts to particular states.

U.S. Department of Energy: Alternative Fuels Data Center (www.eere.energy.gov/afdc/laws/incen_laws.html). A database that captures state and federal laws and incentives related to alternative fuels and vehicles, air quality, fuel efficiency, and other transportation-related topics.

U.S. Department of Energy: Energy Information Administration (www.eia.doe.gov). Documents on climate change from DOE's independent statistical and analysis agency.

Carbon Offset Developers and Validators

Companies that create offset projects (a methane-capture project in China, for example, that creates carbon credits for sale in the European carbon-trading market) and companies that validate those projects (essentially auditors ensuring that the buyer of the carbon credits is actually getting a ton of carbon reductions) are important participants in any carbon-trading scheme. Of course the two services should not reside in the same business entity because of potential conflicts of interest, but the services must work closely together for the market to function effectively. The number of validators are few (it is not a very profitable business) while the number of offset developers are many (there was a distinct gold-rush mentality for several years around the creation of a market for offsets by the United Nations and by EU programs). Information about both can reliably be tracked with these providers and sources:

Carbonfund (www.carbonfund.org). A nonprofit that seeks to make it easy and affordable for any individual, business, or organization to reduce and offset their climate impact and hasten the transition to a clean energy future.

Climate CHECK (www.climate-check.com) The principals at ClimateCHECK authored the ISO 14064 greenhouse gas measurement standards and have also developed the Greenhouse Gas Management Institute to professionalize those who administer GHG accounting. The firm's GHG management services include emissions inventories, buying/selling credits, and making products more climate-friendly.

Native Energy (www.nativeenergy.com). Creates renewable energy projects on tribal lands in North America and customizes offset portfolios for businesses and organizations.

Scientific Certification Systems (www.scscertified.com). Third-party validation and verification of carbon-offset projects to ensure that emission reduction claims are credible, transparent, and tradable in the international carbon market.

TerraPass (www.terrapass.com). Works directly with carbon reduction projects, providing revenue to dairy farms, landfill gas installations, and other projects that yield carbon credits, then sells the credits to individuals and businesses.

The Climate Trust (www.climatetrust.org). Specializes in climate solutions for governments, utilities, and large businesses by providing carbon offsets, customized voluntary offset programs, and climate-consulting services.

Additional Carbon Offset Developers and Re-Sellers

Atmosfair (www.atmosfair.com)

BeGreenNow (www.begreennow.com)

Bonneville Environmental Foundation (www.b-e-f.org)

Brighter Planet (www.brighterplanet.org)

Carbon Catalog (www.carboncatalog.org)

Carbon Neutral Company (www.carbonneutralcompany.com)

Carbon Passport (www.carbonpassport.com)

Drive Neutral (www.driveneutral.org)

GreenWorldApps (www.greenworldapps.com)

Offset Carbon Credits (www.offsetcarboncredits.com)

Sustainable Travel International (www.Sustainabletravel. org)

Sterling Planet (www.sterlingplanet.com)

Carbon Calculators

Part of managing a carbon footprint involves understanding the actions that comprise creating carbon emissions in the first place and subsequently learning what measures effectively reduce those emissions. Prioritizing actions can be tricky without simple ways to measure likely outcomes. Carbon calculators such as those found on the following websites provide back-of-the-envelope metrics:

www.brighterplanet.com
www.climatetrust.org
www.carbonfootprint.com
www.carbonfund.org/business/calculator
www.conservation.org
www.coolclimate.berkeley.edu/
www.earthlab.com
www.jpmorganclimatecare.com/business/business-co2-calculator
www.terrapass.com
www.safeclimate.net/calculator

Carbon Trading and Registries

Trading in regulated carbon allowances or voluntary offset credits can be accomplished by direct business-to-business transactions, but is more typically conducted on exchanges. The following are resources for learning more about existing and future trading platforms.

California Climate Action Registry (www.climateregistry.org). A program of the Climate Action Reserve committed to solving climate change through emissions accounting and reduction.

Chicago Climate Exchange (www.chicagoclimatex.com). Know as CCX, this exchange provides North America's only voluntary cap-and-trade system for all six greenhouse gases with global affiliates and projects worldwide.

Chicago Climate Futures Exchange (www.ccfe.com). Derivatives exchange that currently offers standardized and cleared futures and options contracts on emission allowances and other environmental products. CCFE is a wholly owned subsidiary of CCX.

Emissions Trading Association (www.ieta.org). A nonprofit business organization created in June 1999 to establish a functional international framework for trading in greenhouse gas emission reductions.

European Climate Exchange (www.europeanclimateexchange.com). Launched by CCX in 2005, this is now the leading exchange operating in the European Union Emissions Trading Scheme. Since 2006, CCX and ECX have been owned by Climate Exchange PLC, a publicly traded company listed on the AIM division of the London Stock Exchange.

European Union Greenhouse Gas Emission Trading System (http://ec.europa.eu/environment/climat/emission/index_en.htm). Commenced operation as the largest multicountry, multisector greenhouse gas emission trading system worldwide.

International Climate Action Partnership (www.icapcarbon action.com). Made up of countries and regions that have implemented or are actively pursuing the implementation of carbon markets through mandatory cap-and-trade systems. The partnership provides a forum in which to share experiences and knowledge.

Midwestern Greenhouse Gas Reduction Accord (www. midwesternaccord.org). A regional agreement by states in the U.S. Midwest (and Canadian provinces) that are committed to coordinated programs to reduce greenhouse gas emissions to combat climate change.

Montréal Climate Exchange (www.m-x.ca/accueil_en.php). A joint venture of the Montréal Exchange (MX) and CCX, this exchange trades futures contracts on carbon dioxide equivalent (CO_2e) units.

New Zealand Emissions Trading Scheme (www.climate-change.govt.nz/emissions-trading-scheme/index.html). An emissions trading scheme that introduces a price on greenhouse gases in New Zealand to provide an incentive for people to reduce emissions and enhance forest carbon sequestration.

Regional Greenhouse Gas Initiative (www.rggi.org/home). The first mandatory, market-based effort in the United States to reduce greenhouse gas emissions. Ten Northeastern and Mid-Atlantic states have capped and will reduce CO_2 emissions from the power sector 10 percent below baseline (average of 2002–2004 emissions) by 2018.

Western Climate Initiative (www.westernclimateinitiative. org). A collaboration of U.S. states, Canadian provinces, and Mexican states working together to identify, evaluate, and implement policies to tackle climate change at a regional level, including the creation of an economy-wide cap-and-trade system.

Carbon Standards Developers

Several consultants, government agencies, and nonprofits have established protocols for carbon measurement, reduction efforts, credit trading, and offset programs.

Climate Action Reserve (www.climateactionreserve.org). A national program working to ensure integrity, transparency, and financial value in the U.S. carbon market.

Energy Star (www.energystar.gov). A joint program of the U.S. Environmental Protection Agency and the U.S. Department of Energy helping businesses to save money and protect the environment through energy efficient products and practices.

U.S. Green Building Council (www.usgbc.org). A nonprofit community of leaders working to make green buildings available to everyone within a generation. USGBC is the founder of the LEED standard for measuring high-performing building construction and retrofits.

World Resources Institute (www.wri.org). An environmental think tank whose mission is to move human society to live in ways that protect the earth's environment and its capacity to provide for the needs and aspirations of current and future generations. WRI has developed numerous protocols and standards that have helped businesses and governments align metrics for measuring and reducing carbon emissions.

Carbon Issue Organizations, Associations, and Nonprofit Groups

Numerous trade associations and nonprofit groups have begun to address the issues around climate change and carbon regulation as they relate to their members. Several useful sources in this category include the following.

Campus Climate Challenge (www.climatechallenge.org). A project of dozens of youth organizations throughout the United States and Canada, focused on mobilizing clean energy activism for educational institutions and companies.

Carbon Markets and Investors Association (www.cmia.net). An international trade association representing firms that finance, invest in, and support activities that reduce emissions. CMIA's members accounted for 75 percent of the global carbon market in 2009, valued at $130 billion in carbon trades.

ClimateWise (www.climatewise.org.uk). A collaborative insurance initiative through which members aim to work together to respond to the myriad risks and opportunities of climate change.

Climate Action Network (http://www.climatenetwork.org). A worldwide network of more than 450 nongovernmental organizations (NGOs) working to promote government and individual action in order to limit human-induced climate change to ecologically sustainable levels.

Climate Justice (www.climatelaw.org). Works to enforce climate change law and provide information about international litigation involving global warming.

Climate Protection Initiative (http://climate.wri.org/project_text.cfm?ProjectID=197). Information on policies and business strategies for achieving strong climate protection goals. CPI is a joint effort between the World Resources Institute and private firms.

Conservation International (www.conservation.org). Programs combine scientific knowledge with expertise in specialized fields to achieve conservation solutions. Their programs work to demonstrate the value of partnerships, lend advice on best practices, and guide implementation of conservation solutions in the field.

Environmental Defense (www.environmentaldefense.org). A national nonprofit organization bringing together experts in science, law, and economics to tackle complex environmental issues, including climate change. Environmental Defense is credited with helping to design the world's first environmental credit-trading market.

Environmental Markets Association (www.environmentalmarkets.org). A U.S.-based trade association focused on promoting market solutions as the most effective strategy to combat environmental issues.

Global Green USA (www.globalgreen.org). A national environmental organization addressing global climate change by creating green buildings and cities.

Innovation Center for Energy and Transportation (iCET) (www.icet.org.cn and www.greencarchina.org and www. ChinaClimateRegistry.org) A Chinese NGO that operates in both China and the U.S. to build public-private partnerships that demonstrate the benefits of low carbon economic development. ICET has been instrumental in applying several California carbon polices to China's climate change efforts, including the Low Carbon Fuel Standard and the creation of a carbon registry for emitters.

Local Governments for Sustainability (www.iclei.org). An international association of local, national, and regional governments that have made a commitment to sustainable development.

Institutional Investors Group on Climate Change (www. iigcc.org/home). A forum for collaboration on climate change for European investors.

Presidential Climate Action Partnership (www.climate actionproject.com). Has developed a comprehensive, non-partisan plan for presidential leadership rooted in climate science and designed to ignite innovation at every level of the American economy.

The Climate Group (www.theclimategroup.org). A nonprofit organization dedicated to advancing business and government leadership on climate change internationally.

United Nations Environment Programme Finance Initiative (www.unepfi.org/about/index.html). A global partnership between the UN Environment Programme (UNEP) and the global financial sector to provide investment in sustainable development projects globally.

United Nations Framework Convention on Climate Change (http://unfccc.int/2860.php). As discussed in more detail throughout this book, most countries signed the international treaty—the UN Framework Convention on Climate Change (UNFCCC)—to take action to address climate change.

U.S. Mayors Climate Protection Agreement (www.usmayors. org/climateprotection). A voluntary group of mayors who have pledged to meet the goals of global climate agreements.

GLOSSARY

Adaptation fund. A fund that was established in January 2002 (COP7, Marrakech) to help developing countries meet the cost of adapting to climate change.

Additionality. A carbon offset project is additional if it can be demonstrated that in the absence of the project, (a) the proposed voluntary measure would not be implemented, or (b) the mandatory policy/regulation would be systematically not enforced and that noncompliance with those requirements is widespread in the country/region, or (c) the project will lead to a greater level of enforcement of the existing mandatory policy/regulation.

Allocation. The process by which emissions allowances are initially distributed under an emissions cap-and-trade system. Authorizations to emit can initially be distributed in a number of ways. See auctioning, benchmarking, grandfathering, and updating.

Allowance. A government-issued authorization to emit a certain amount of greenhouse gas. In greenhouse gas markets, an allowance is commonly denominated as one ton of CO_2e per year. See also "permit" and "credits" (aka "carbon credits"). The total number of allowances allocated to all entities in a cap-and-trade system is determined by the size of the overall cap on emissions.

Annex I countries. Developed countries that, under the Kyoto Protocol, have accepted greenhouse gas emission reduction obligations and must submit an annual greenhouse gas inventory.

Assembly Bill 32/AB32 (also known as the Global Warming Solutions Act of 2006). The California law setting up the first enforceable statewide program in the United States to cap all greenhouse gas emissions from major industries. The law requires that by 2020 the state's greenhouse gas emissions be reduced to 1990 levels.

Assigned amount unit (AAUs). Allowances issued to Annex I countries that have a cap on their emissions under the Kyoto Protocol. Each AAU grants the country the right to emit one ton of greenhouse gases during a given commitment period.

Auctioning. Distribution of carbon emission allowances through the receipt of bids from potential buyers with allowances sold to the highest bidder.

Banking. The ability to carry over unused carbon credits from one commitment period of a trading scheme to another commitment period.

Baseline. Emissions are forecasted under a business-as-usual scenario. Also called baseline scenario.

Benchmarking. Distribution of emission allowances on the basis of relative emissions per unit of output (see also "intensity approach"). Benchmarking may also refer to the year used as the starting point for a company or country, against which future carbon reduction goals are set.

Borrowing. The use of carbon credits due to be allocated in the future to enable regulated entities to meet their target in an earlier time period.

Business-as-usual (BAU). A scenario in which things are done in the usual way; under BAU future carbon emissions are estimated in the absence of a project or changes in current policies to reduce emissions.

California Air Resources Board (CARB). The government agency established by California's legislature in 1967 to attain and maintain healthy air quality, conduct research into the causes of and solutions to air pollution, and systematically attack the serious problem caused by motor vehicles. CARB is the chief implementing agency for Assembly Bill 32 (AB32).

California Climate Action Registry (CCAR). A nonprofit voluntary registry for greenhouse gas emissions in California and the official registry for AB32. The purpose of the registry is to help companies and organizations with operations in the state to establish GHG emission baselines against which any future GHG emission reduction requirements may be applied.

Cap-and-trade. Cap-and-trade is part of an emissions trading system created to reduce the amount of greenhouse gas emissions (GHGs). The regulating entity determines a price on emitting greenhouse gases and establishes a limit or cap on the amount of greenhouse gas emissions that may be produced each year. The cap is gradually lowered, thereby requiring greater emissions reductions over time. Cap-and-trade works by creating a supply and demand for carbon. When there is a shortage of allowances, the price will be driven up, thereby creating a financial incentive for firms to cut their emissions.

Carbon. Shorthand for carbon dioxide (CO_2) and often used to refer to all six greenhouse gases.

Carbon capture and storage (CCS). A process consisting of the separation of CO_2 from industrial- and energy-related sources, transport to a storage location, and long-term isolation from the atmosphere. CO_2 may be stored underground in depleted oil and gas fields, noncommercial coal fields, and saline aquifers. It may also be injected into the ocean. Also known as carbon capture and geological storage (CCGS), or carbon capture and sequestration.

Carbon dioxide equivalent (CO_2e). Carbon dioxide equivalents provide a universal standard of measurement against which the impacts of releasing (or avoiding the release of) different greenhouse gases can be evaluated. Every greenhouse gas has a Global Warming Potential (GWP), a measurement of the impact that particular gas has on "radiative forcing," that is, the additional heat/energy which is retained in the Earth's ecosystem through the addition of this gas to the atmosphere. For example, carbon dioxide has a GWP of one; sulphur hexafluoride has a GWP of 23,900.

Carbon footprint. The amount of greenhouse gases produced in a given period through direct or indirect emissions of carbon by an individual, a company (or a company's installations), or a nation, and measured in tons of carbon dioxide equivalent (see CO_2e).

Carbon gravity. The concept that the most cost-effective methods for reducing carbon emissions have the lowest negative cost and that such measures can be repaid from saving money that is currently being wasted (for example, replacing inefficient lighting with energy-saving fixtures and bulbs, and paying for the upgrades with savings on electricity bills).

Carbon resilience. The ability of a company to adapt to paying for carbon emissions that were previously emitted at no cost; to adapt to a supply chain that will require carbon disclosures and add carbon costs of its own; and the ability to profit from low-carbon products and services within a company that may previously have had little or no value.

Carbon sink. Natural or human-made systems that absorb carbon dioxide from the atmosphere and store them. Forests are the most common form of sink, in addition to soils, peat, permafrost, ocean water, and carbonate deposits in the ocean.

Carbon tax. A surcharge on the carbon content of fossil fuels that aims to discourage their use and thereby reduce carbon dioxide emissions.

Carbon tipping point. The time at which a company, that is largely unregulated as it pertains to carbon, will switch from paying little or nothing for carbon emissions to one that must respond to new regulations and costs on carbon emissions.

Certification. A process by which a greenhouse gas reduction project is audited by a government agency or independent authority to determine if it meets established criteria; for instance, approving emission reductions from a carbon project and, as a result, issuing emission-reduction credits to the entity that owns the project.

Certified Emission Reduction (CERs). Carbon credits arising from Clean Development Mechanism projects. One CER is awarded for a reduction in greenhouse gas emissions equivalent in impact to one ton of carbon dioxide.

Chicago Climate Exchange (CCX). Voluntary cap-and-trade scheme that started trading in 2003. Members make a voluntary commitment to reduce carbon emissions. Among the members are companies from North America, municipalities, U.S. states, and universities. The CCX also certifies and trades offset credits under its own standards.

Clean Air Act (CAA). United States federal legislation, first passed in 1963, relating to the reduction of smog and air pollution in general. The Clean Air Act Amendments of 1990 proposed emissions trading, added provisions for addressing acid rain, ozone depletion and toxic air pollution, and established a national emissions permit program. The CAA provides grounds for the USEPA to regulate carbon emissions, a responsibility that was affirmed by the U.S. Supreme Court in 2007.

Clean Development Mechanism (CDM). An arrangement under the UNFCCC's Kyoto Protocol allowing industrialized countries (Annex I countries) with a greenhouse gas reduction commitment to invest in projects that reduce emissions in developing countries (non-Annex I countries) as an alternative to more expensive emission reductions in their own countries.

Commitment period. The time frame used by regulators in which a source of carbon emissions (by an installation or country) is required to achieve specified emissions reductions. Under the Kyoto Protocol, the first commitment period was five years (from calendar year 2008 to calendar year-end 2012). Other regulatory systems use a three-year commitment period (see "RGGI," for example).

Community international transaction log. The European Union's independent transaction log records the issue, transfer, and cancellation of EU Allowances within the European Union and monitors compliance with Kyoto Protocol rules on the issuance, transfer, and cancellation of these allowances.

Compliance market. Another term for a mandatory cap-and-trade program in which a country sets legally binding caps on GHG emissions.

Conference of the Parties (COP). The COP is the supreme body of the UNFCCC. It meets once a year, in a different member country, to review the progress of various agreements reached by member nations.

Control share. A source of emissions, for which one company or installation is entirely responsible (see also "equity share").

Crediting period. The duration for which a project generates carbon credits. Under most trading systems, the crediting period may not extend beyond the operational lifetime of the project.

Designated National Authority (DNA). The government office that provides national approval for CDM project participation, whether as a project owner or as an investor. The DNA issues the Letter of Approval (LoA) required for registration of a project. Projects need both host country approval and investor country approval.

Designated Operational Entity (DOE). A legal entity accredited by the CDM executive board to carry out the validation, verification, and/or certification of CDM projects.

Double counting. A potential problem that can arise when the same emissions reductions are counted toward more than one reduction obligation. It may occur when carbon reductions are achieved at one point on a supply chain, but multiple steps on the chain try to take ownership of the reductions. Double counting can also occur when emissions reductions are counted against the targets/obligations of both local and national carbon reduction schemes (or national and international schemes).

Downstream system. Also known as a "source-based," a system in which the point of regulation coincides with the point of emission of covered greenhouse gases. Examples of a source-based approach include the Regional Greenhouse Gas Initiative's cap on power plant CO_2 emissions or the cap on large industrial sources in the European Union's Emissions Trading Scheme. (See also "upstream".)

Emissions cap. A mandatory limit, in a scheduled time frame that puts a "ceiling" on the total amount of anthropogenic greenhouse gas emissions that can be released into the atmosphere.

Emissions trading. The process or policy that allows the buying and selling of credits or allowances created under an emissions cap.

Emission reduction unit (ERUs). Carbon credits arising from Joint Implementation projects. One ERU is awarded for a reduction in greenhouse gas emissions equivalent in impact to one ton of carbon dioxide.

Equity share. A source of emissions, for which multiple companies or installations are responsible. (See also "control share".)

European Union allowance unit (EUAs). Allowances issued to installations which have a cap on their emissions under the EU Emission Trading Scheme. Each EUA grants the installation the right to emit one ton of carbon dioxide during a commitment period.

European Union Emissions Trading Scheme (EU ETS). The world's largest greenhouse gas emissions trading system is the European Union's Emissions Trading Scheme, which limits CO_2 emissions from approximately 12,000 installations in the 27 EU member states. Launched in 2005, the ETS covers electricity and major industrial sectors that together produce nearly half the EU's CO_2 emissions.

Flexible mechanisms (or flexibility mechanisms). Countries with commitments under the Kyoto Protocol to limit or reduce greenhouse gas emissions must meet their targets primarily through national measures. However, the Kyoto Protocol allows for three "flexible mechanisms": emissions trading (ET); the Clean Development Mechanism (CDM); and Joint Implementation (JI). These measures comprise what is known as the carbon market.

GHG. See "greenhouse gases."

Global warming potential (GWP). All greenhouse gases have what is called a Global Warming Potential (GWP). This value is used to compare the abilities of different greenhouse gases to trap heat in the atmosphere. GWPs are based on the heat-absorbing ability of each gas relative to that of carbon dioxide (CO_2), as well as to the decay rate of each gas (the amount removed from the atmosphere over a given number of years). GWPs can also be used to define the impact greenhouse gases will have on global warming over different time periods or time horizons. (See also "CO_2e".)

Gold standard. Created by several nonprofit organizations and Helio International in 2003, the Gold Standard offers project developers a tool with which they can ensure that CDM, JI, and VER projects have real environmental benefits and, in so doing, give confidence to host countries and the public that projects represent new and additional investments in measurable carbon reductions.

Grandfathering. Distribution of emission allowances to installations that emit carbon pollution, usually free of charge, on the basis of historic emissions.

Green tags (also called renewable energy certificates or RECs). A form of credit created when a renewable energy facility produces electricity under a government mandate to produce clean energy, such as a Renewable Portfolio Standard. These credits are traded, like stocks, through brokers. Buyers of the credits are in effect supporting the production of renewable energy, often without directly using the energy produced. In the United States, one credit represents the proof that one megawatt-hour (MWh) of electricity was generated from an eligible renewable energy source.

Greenhouse gases (GHGs). These gases contribute to the warming of the Earth's atmosphere by absorbing and emitting radiation from the Earth's surface. Some GHGs occur naturally in the atmosphere, while others result from human activities. Appendix A describes the six GHGs in more detail.

Greenhouse Gas Protocol (GHGP). The most widely used international accounting tool for government and businesses to understand, quantify, and manage greenhouse gas emissions. The GHGP is a partnership between the World Resources Institute and the World Business Council for Sustainable Development.

Host country. A country where a JI or CDM project is physically located. A project has to be approved by the host country to receive CERs or ERUs.

Installation. A stationary source of carbon dioxide emissions, such as a boiler or refinery stack, that is regulated under an emissions trading scheme.

Intensity approach. Quantifying carbon emissions from a source or a country by measuring the total carbon emissions divided by a chosen unit of production. Sometimes referred to as "benchmarking." (See also "nominal approach".)

Intergovernmental Panel on Climate Change (IPCC). The scientific body mandated by the UN to evaluate the risk of climate change caused by human activity. The IPCC publishes special reports on topics relevant to the implementation of the UNFCCC.

International Transaction Log (ITL). A centralized database of all tradable credits under the Kyoto Protocol. Its main purpose is to verify all international transactions and their compliance with rules and policies of the Kyoto Protocol.

Joint implementation (JI). A mechanism through which Annex I countries can invest in emission-reduction projects (Joint Implementation Projects) in any other Annex I country as an alternative to reducing emissions domestically.

Kyoto Protocol. The agreement reached at the COP3 meeting in Kyoto in 1997 by UNFCCC members that committed developed countries and countries making the transition to a market economy (Annex I countries) to achieve quantified targets for decreasing their emissions of greenhouse gases.

Leakage. An increase of greenhouse gas emissions outside the boundaries of a project or a region that has a cap on emissions which is caused by that cap. Leakage effectively reduces the net greenhouse gas emissions reductions from that region or project. For example, one region may limit emissions from a power plant, but factories within that region may switch to electricity from polluting power plants outside the region and thereby "leak" the carbon emissions from the regulated region to the unregulated one with no net improvement in GHG emissions overall.

Letter of approval (LoA). Letter issued by a designated national authority authorizing an entity to become a CDM project participant.

Linking. Authorization by the regulator for entities covered under a cap-and-trade program to use allowances or offsets from a different jurisdiction's regulatory regime (such as another cap-and-trade program) for compliance purposes. Linking may expand opportunities for low-cost emission reductions, resulting in lower compliance costs.

Load-based system. A system in which the covered emitters are electricity retailers responsible for all the emissions associated with the generation of the electricity they provide to customers, including electricity imported from other states, thus avoiding problems of leakage. (See also "Leakage".)

Low Carbon Fuel Standards (LCFS). The LCFS requires fuel providers to ensure that the mix of fuel they sell in the market meets, on average, a declining target for greenhouse gas emissions measured in grams of carbon dioxide equivalent per unit of fuel energy sold. By 2020, the California LCFS mandates a 10 percent reduction in the carbon intensity of fuel production and use within California.

Midwestern Greenhouse Gas Reduction Accord (MGGRA). A regional agreement by governors of the states in the U.S. Midwest and one Canadian province that establishes a multisector cap-and-trade program to reduce greenhouse gas emissions.

Monitoring. The collection and archiving of all relevant data necessary for determining the baseline, and measuring anthropogenic emissions by sources of greenhouse gases within the project boundary of a project activity and leakage, as applicable.

National Allocation Plan. Defines the basis on how emission allowances to individual installations are allocated under the EU Emission Trading Scheme.

Nominal approach. Quantifying carbon emissions from a source or a country, solely by measuring the actual emissions. (See also "intensity approach".)

Non-Annex I countries. Developing countries that have no greenhouse gas emission reduction obligations under Kyoto but may participate in the Clean Development Mechanism.

Offsets. offsets enable individuals and businesses to reduce the greenhouse gas emissions they are responsible for by offsetting, reducing or displacing the CO_2 in another place, typically where it is more economical to do so. Carbon offsets typically include renewable energy, energy efficiency and reforestation projects. Emission reductions are usually calculated by reference to a business-as-usual baseline.

Over-the-counter (OTC)market. Trades arranged by brokers, as opposed to trades on exchanges or bilateral (direct) trades.

Permit. Permits are often used for denoting carbon credits, since these credits grant the owner the right to emit greenhouse gases.

Price cap. An upper limit set on the price of traded emissions allowances so that they cannot exceed a predetermined price; also known as a safety valve.

Primary CERs. Carbon credits issued to or bought directly from a CDM project. In general, the buyer of primary CERs is exposed to the project risks. (See also "Certified Emission Reduction".)

Project design document. Describes the characteristics of a CDM or JI project, completed by project developers in order to register their project. Project developers have to submit this document to register their CDM or JI project.

Project participant. An organization involved in a CDM project as a project owner or investor. Project participants determine the allocation of CERs issued to a CDM project.

Reduced Emissions from Deforestation and Degradation (REDD). Mitigation action that seeks to preserve existing carbon stocks in forests (typically tropical rainforests), peat lands, and so forth. The approach would be additional to project-based efforts such as the CDM. Carbon credits issued for REDD projects have been controversial, due to issues such as the permanence of the projects, leakage, adequate monitoring, and baseline assumptions.

Regional Greenhouse Gas Initiative (RGGI). A regional cap-and-trade program for Northeastern and Mid-Atlantic states of the United States that began operations in 2009 covering only power plants.

Registration. The formal acceptance by the CDM executive board of the eligibility of a project to earn CERs.

Registry. An electronic database that acts as the official repository of carbon credits and serves as a tracking system for the transfer of such credits.

Removal unit (RMU). Carbon credits relating to land use, land use change and forestry activities in Annex 1 countries that reduce or sequester emissions. Each RMU is equal to one metric ton of CO_2 equivalent.

Scope 1, 2, 3. Carbon emissions are divided into three categories or "scopes." Scope 1 includes an installation's direct emissions (a boiler at a factory, for example); Scope 2 includes indirect emissions created on behalf of an installation (such as electricity generated by a local utility for use at the installation); and Scope 3, emissions that are not clearly the responsibility of a given installation, but which may be reasonably attributed to it (air travel for a sales force, for instance).

Secondary market. The second transaction or trading of a carbon credit. In a secondary market, buyers purchase credits from other buyers rather than the original issuing entity.

Sequestration. A technique for the permanent storage of carbon dioxide or other greenhouse gases so that they will not be released into the atmosphere where they would contribute to the greenhouse effect. Examples include forestry or geologic sequestration of carbon dioxide through its injection and storage underground.

Small-scale projects. Those that can use a simplified process for CDM registration. Those eligible are renewable energy projects under 15 MW, energy-efficiency projects that reduce energy consumption by up to 15 GWh per year, or project activities that emit less than 15 kilo tons CO_2 equivalent per year.

Supplementarity. A provision in the Kyoto Protocol that requires use of the flexibility mechanisms to be supplementary to domestic action to reduce emissions.

The Climate Registry (TCR). A collaboration between states and provinces in the United States, Canada, and Mexico aimed at developing and managing a common GHG emissions reporting system. The registry supports various greenhouse gas emission reporting and reduction policies for its member states and reporting entities. TCR hopes to become the national standard under a U.S. federal cap-and-trade scheme.

Ton. Greenhouse gas emissions are measured in tons, which is actually the weight of the fuel used to create the gas (or its equivalent).

United Nations Framework Convention on Climate Change (UNFCCC). The UNFCCC sets an overall framework for international efforts to fight against climate change. Its main objective is "stabilization of greenhouse gas concentrations in the atmosphere at a level that would prevent dangerous anthropogenic (human-made) interference with the climate system." It was established in 1992 at the Rio Earth Summit.

Upstream system. An upstream approach to a cap-and-trade system matches the point of regulation with the point of entry of fossil fuels into commerce within the covered region. (See also "Downstream".)

Validation. An independent evaluation of a CDM project by a Designated Operational Entity to ensure its conformity to the requirements of a CDM project.

Verification. Each year, regulated entities are required to report the amount of emissions that have been emitted in the previous year. This information must be reported and verified by a designated operational entity (DOE) and the reports made public. If an operator's emission reports are not deemed satisfactory, they will not be permitted to sell allowances until a verified report is approved.

Voluntary carbon market. Voluntary markets operate in countries, including the United States, that have do not have a mandatory cap-and-trade program. These markets are often referred to as the "unregulated" markets. In general, credits created in the voluntary market have less stringent control mechanisms and as a result are priced lower than credits in the regulated compliance market.

Western Climate Initiative (WCI). A regional initiative launched in February 2007 by states and provinces along the western rim of the United States, Canada, and Mexico. The initiative looks to develop a multisector cap-and-trade system covering 90 percent of the emissions from member jurisdictions. WCI is expected to launch in 2012, and the proposed target is to reduce greenhouse gas emissions by 15 percent below 2005 levels by 2020.

White tags (also called energy-efficiency credits). A document which certifies that a certain reduction of energy consumption has been attained. Each tag represents one megawatt hour of energy savings. Once a white tag is created, the tag can be retained or sold in regulated or unregulated environmental credit markets.

APPENDIX A

Carbon 101: The Four Key Facts

In recent years, there has been much political debate about whether global warming is real, whether it is largely human-caused, and whether it will be a significant economic change factor. In truth, these questions are somewhat irrelevant, because policy changes have already occurred in much of the developed world, putting a price on carbon, and decarbonizing a business is a matter of reducing wasteful uses of energy, something that saves money regardless of laws or value judgments.

The cause of climate change is simple: carbon dioxide (CO_2), much of it coming from the combustion of fossil fuels, is trapped in the atmosphere which acts like a greenhouse, holding the heat inside and building up the temperature over time. Unlike a greenhouse, however, you can't open a window in the atmosphere to vent the trapped CO_2 when it gets too warm, so we are now seeing ice caps melt and sea levels rise, heat waves and hurricanes of greater intensity and duration in some places, drought in others, and disease-bearing pests moving to places they previously avoided.

These effects are not just "warming." A more accurate term for the results of this CO_2 blanket is "climate change." We will soon see changes in ocean currents and temperatures, which, like our body's bloodstream, are the planet's primary heating and cooling systems and will therefore have even more unpredictable and catastrophic effects. While scientists argue over the fine details of exactly what, when, where, and how much, there are four key facts that are not in dispute:

1. Carbon dioxide (CO_2) is the primary "greenhouse gas." Before the Industrial Age began about 150 years ago, the concentration of CO_2 in Earth's atmosphere had remained between 180 and 280 parts per million ("ppm") for at least 200,000 years. There are five other greenhouse gases (often referred to as "GHGs," but in this book, the generic term "carbon" is used, described in table A.1). Each of these gases traps warmth at different rates and are therefore expressed as CO_2e (carbon dioxide equivalents). Each gas has a "global warming potential" that is expressed compared to the heat-trapping abilities of CO_2.

2. There is agreement that the level of CO_2e is over 380 ppm today and climbing annually. These first two points are not subject to debate, because they have been measured.

3. This dramatic increase in CO_2e coincides with humans manufacturing new chemicals with global warming potential and the burning of fossil fuels at a prodigious rate.

4. Even if we could suddenly stop dumping tons of CO_2e into the atmosphere every day from our cars and power plants we would still suffer serious consequences over the next half-century from what our parents and grandparents put into the atmosphere. Yes, the CO_2 from my grandfather's Oldsmobile is still hovering above us. That's because CO_2 in the atmosphere can't go anywhere, nor can it be consumed rapidly enough by trees and other plants, which absorb CO_2 and emit oxygen—the opposite of animals, including humans, which take in oxygen and exhale CO_2.

Table A.1 The six greenhouse gases and their characteristics

Greenhouse Gas	GWP	DESCRIPTION
Carbon Dioxide (CO_2):	1	CO_2 is produced naturally by living organisms and by the burning of fossil fuels. Carbon accounts for the largest share of U.S. greenhouse gas emissions.
Nitrous Oxide (N_2O):	310 times that of CO_2	Nitrous oxide is a naturally occurring gas that is released through both natural and anthropogenic processes and is considered a major GHG not because of its quantity but because of its GWP. The largest source of N_2O is agricultural soils, where microbial processes, application of fertilizers, nitrogen-fixing crops and other factors emitted 70% of U.S. N_2O emissions in 1998. Other sources include fossil fuel combustion, acid production, manure management, human sewage, and waste combustion.
Methane:	Approximately 21 times that of CO_2	Methane is a naturally occurring gas, considered to be the second most dangerous GHG because of its abundance and GWP. Methane comes from coal formations, landfills, livestock digestive processes, decomposing waste, and wetland rice cultivation.
Hydrofluorocarbon Gases (HFC):	140 to 11,700 times that of CO_2	These gases are manmade and were developed largely as an alternative to ozone-damaging chlorofluorocarbons (CFC). They are banned under the 1987 Montreal Protocol. HFCs do not damage the ozone layer, but they do contribute to global warming. They are used largely in refrigeration and in semi-conductor manufacturing.
Perfluorocarbons (PFC):	7,400 times that of CO_2	PFCs are a by-product of aluminum smelting and uranium enriching and were manufactured to replace CFCs in making semi-conductors.
Sulphur Hexafluoride (SF_6):	23,900 times that of CO_2	Largely used in heavy industry to insulate high-voltage equipment and to assist the manufacturing of cable cooling systems.

Sources: U.S. Energy Information Agency, International Energy Agency, Intergovernmental Panel on Climate Change.

There are two reasons the world's plants can't keep up with consuming the amount of CO_2 we are emitting. We're discharging more CO_2 than ever before and, perhaps more to the point, we're cutting down trees and clearing forestlands at an equally prodigious rate, depleting the very life forms that might save us from our shortsightedness. Adding insult to injury, to clear the land for agriculture, many countries with rainforests are burning the vegetation, the combustion of which simply releases more CO_2 into the atmosphere.

Just how much carbon are we pumping into the atmosphere each year and how fast are we adding more on a net basis? Carbon emissions (all six regulated greenhouse gases) are measured in "tons," which is actually the weight of the fuel used to create the harmful gas (or its equivalent). For example, a gallon of gasoline contains about five pounds of carbon. When you burn it in your engine, you release the five pounds. Do that 400 times and you've just dumped a ton of CO_2 into the atmosphere. A more direct example is dry ice, which is simply frozen CO_2. As a ton of dry ice evaporates, it releases that ton of pure CO_2 into the atmosphere.

Globally, emissions in the first decade of the twenty-first century averaged about 30 billion metric tons per year...

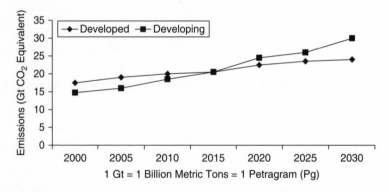

Figure A.2   Trends in GHG emissions over time

...and are growing by a net of about three billion tons annually from two primary sources as shown in table A.3. The ocean absorbs up to a third of this excess CO_2, but acidifies seawater in the process and therefore disturbs critical links in the marine food chain, killing off plant and animal life that humans and wildlife rely upon for sustenance.

To put these figures in context, the United States is home to about 5 percent of the world's population, but it produces over 20 percent of the world's net annual excess greenhouse gases.

Table A.3   Sources of carbon added to the atmosphere annually

CO_2 source (worldwide)	CO_2 increase (metric tons annually)
Burning fossil fuels	+5.5 billion
Deforestation	+1.5 billion
Ocean absorption	−2.0 billion
Terrestrial plant life absorption	−2.0 billion
NET ANNUAL CO_2e INCREASE	3.0 billion tons

A typical American motorist driving 12,000 miles per year burns 600 gallons of gasoline or 1.5 tons of carbon. The emissions from all American passenger vehicles exceed the total national CO_2 emissions of all but three countries. The average American uses 12,000 kilowatt-hours of electricity, and if that electricity comes from a coal-fired power plant, each kilowatt-hour creates two pounds of carbon emissions or six tons of carbon per person per year.

These measurable, undisputed facts about climate change persuaded the likes of Governor Schwarzenegger, Prime Minister Blair, and CEO Darbee to take action to cut carbon emissions, largely because of the unprecedented scientific consensus that delivered these facts. The United Nations Intergovernmental Panel on Climate Change (IPCC) assembles scientists from 130 countries and publishes a summary of peer-reviewed research every five or six years. Nothing gets into the summary that does not have the agreement of 100 percent of these scientists. There is no other field of scientific inquiry that benefits from this remarkable degree of collaboration and consensus. The result was a Nobel Prize for the IPCC in 2007, the same year that Al Gore collected his award.

These scientists also agree that if emissions exceed 450 ppm, the effects become more severe and less predictable. As a result, many policymakers have aimed at reducing emissions to a level that avoids that "tipping point." Other scientists recommend a limit based on the resulting temperature rise, suggesting we can't afford an average global increase of more than two degrees centigrade. These metrics are important to the Carbon Code, because policy makers use them to decide on carbon-reduction targets and timing.

Finally, the scientific community is not alone in making omi-
nous, if not precisely timed, predictions about the impacts of climate change. In an October 2003 report, entitled "An Abrupt
Climate Change Scenario and Its Implications for U.S. National
Security," Pentagon researchers examined the destabilizing effects
of large-scale floods, famine, disease, crop failure, and human
displacement, among other foreseeable consequences of global
warming. The fact that the Pentagon studied the implications of
these outcomes, or that they believed the scientists who described
the possibilities, is not as remarkable as the fact that the paper
presents these outcomes as unavoidable.

Sources

"Carbon Dioxide Record from the Hawaiian Mauna Loa Observatory from NOAA's
    Climate Monitoring and Diagnostics Laboratory," http://www.cmdl.noaa.gov/
    info/testimony.html, accessed December 28, 2009.
"Carbon Emissions from an Average Coal-Fired Power Plant," http://www.eia.
    doe.gov/cneaf/electricity/page/co2_report/co2report.html#electric, accessed
    November 25, 2009.
Epstein, Paul R., and Jesse Selber. *Oil: A Life Cycle Analysis of its Health and Environmental
    Impacts,* The Center for Health and the Global Environment, Harvard Medical
    School, March 2002.
"Global Greenhouse Gas Data," USEPA, http://www.epa.gov/climatechange/index.
    html, accessed December 22, 2009.
Global Population Profile: 2002, United States Department of Commerce, Agency for
    International Development, Bureau for Global Health, March 2004, A-10.
International Energy-Related Environmental Information—Carbon Dioxide Emissions,
    United States Department of Energy, Energy Information Administration,
    November 2004.
Pickrell, John. "Oceans Found to Absorb Half of All Man-Made Carbon Dioxide,"
    National Geographic News, July 15, 2004.
Tamminen, Terry. *Lives Per Gallon: The True Cost of Our Oil Addiction* (Washington,
    DC: Island Press, 2008).
Tamminen, Terry, Sasha Abelson, and Kristina Haddad. *Climate Change Handbook*
    (Santa Monica: Seventh Generation Advisors Press, 2009).

APPENDIX B

The United Nations Framework Convention on Climate Change (UNFCCC) and the Kyoto Protocol

The most cursory review of carbon policy to date will high-light the Kyoto Protocol and related efforts made by the United Nations to address the issue with a global agreement. Nations around the world realized that such an agreement was necessary to balance the needs of developed countries (those that had already built wealth and prosperity by burning fossil fuels and leaving the atmosphere crowded with the resulting carbon waste) and the developing countries (those that were struggling to catch up economically and were using the cheapest forms of energy to do so—more fossil fuels). What if one nation spent heavily on decarbonizing its economy and others did not? Would the businesses of that nation suffer a competitive disadvantage from policies or taxes imposed by its government alone, while others making no such efforts avoided new costs indefinitely?

Diplomats from both developed and developing countries looked to two prior examples that offered lessons for tackling these challenges presented by climate change, in particular the organizing framework addressing global emissions of gasses depleting the world's ozone layer and the market approach that was solving the SO_2/acid rain problems.

The Ozone Solution as a Model for Carbon

In the early 1980s, rookie congressman Al Gore persuaded his colleagues to hold the first hearing on the subject of climate change. It had been almost impossible to get serious attention to the matter and certainly nothing close to the consensus around the effects of SO_2 pollution. Fred Krupp of Environmental Defense, one of the architects of the cap-and-trade approach to dealing with SO_2, and others soon realized that without a global agreement, essentially an international Clean Air Act, there could be no similar outcome and the climate problem might never be solved.

As often happens with monumental discoveries, this one began with a humble researcher who was looking for something else. José Mario Molina-Pasquel Henríquez was born in Mexico City in the middle of World War II, the son of his country's ambassador to Ethiopia. Although he didn't follow his father into international diplomacy, he did study in Europe and the United States before settling into teaching and research at the University of California Irvine, just south of Los Angeles.

Scientists had long been concerned over a growing hole in the ozone layer of Earth's atmosphere, their unease made more acute by a lack of any credible explanation for the phenomenon. Although corrosive to lungs at ground level, ozone in the upper atmosphere filters out harmful ultraviolet rays that would otherwise cause much more deadly skin cancers. In 1974, Molina and a colleague published an article in the journal *Nature* that fingered the chemicals used in refrigerators and air conditioners— CFCs—as the culprits.

Although some scientists were skeptical, politicians and the public were even more unconvinced because chemical giant DuPont poured money into a PR campaign to cast doubt on Molina's findings. As evidence mounted from a wide variety of sources that validated his conclusion, Molina gave talks around the world calling for the elimination of these harmful pollutants. By 1987, world leaders convened in Montreal under United Nations auspices to do just that. They inked a deal setting a target that by 1996 "consumption and production of (CFCs) does not exceed zero."

DuPont fought back, trying to convince U.S. regulators to overturn the agreement, while quietly putting its own scientists to work to find nontoxic alternatives to CFCs. Within a year, DuPont changed its tune. Having invented several alternatives, the chemical giant was now poised to profit handsomely from the ban on its own legacy products.

In 1995, Mario Molina was awarded the Nobel prize for his earth-shaking discovery and successful advocacy. In 2003, DuPont was awarded the National Medal of Technology, recognizing the company as the leader in developing CFC replacements. In September 2009, the Montreal Protocol on Substances that Deplete the Ozone Layer celebrated its twenty-second birthday. Every UN member country has ratified the treaty, the first time that has happened with any international environmental agreement. Concentrations of harmful gases are dropping and the ozone hole is expected to be "healed" by 2050.

Although it was rapidly becoming apparent that the Montreal Protocol could become a model for tackling carbon emissions, there was no Fred Krupp or C. Boyden Gray in a position to champion that approach (as those two had done for Clean Air Act amendments to create a cap-and-trade system for SO_2 pollution). The leadership for this international version of the Clean Air Act came from a very unlikely source.

Gro Harlem Brundtland was born a few months before Germany invaded Poland and ignited World War II. Like many Norwegian children of modest, hard-working families, she got good grades at school, earning a spot at a university and a medical degree in the year President Kennedy was assassinated and the Cold War raged between Russia, the United States, and their respective allies. Brundtland was a good enough student to earn a spot at Harvard, where she took a master's degree in public health.

Although she returned to her homeland to practice as a doctor in Oslo's public schools, her experiences led her to another kind of public service: politics. She became active in a new movement that linked human illness to environmental pollution, with a growing body of scientific evidence that contributed to the formation of the USEPA in 1970, on the heels of the first Earth Day. Because Brundtland was both a respected medical academic and practitioner, people around the world listened to her. By 1974, she was appointed Norway's Minister for Environmental Affairs. Six years later she had built such a following that she was elected her nation's first and only female prime minister.

Her influence at the crossroads of politics and environmental science led her to an even bigger stage. In 1983 Brundtland chaired the World Commission on Environment and Development for the United Nations, the so-called "Brundtland Commission," and wrestled governments worldwide to a shared understanding of the problems facing the rapidly growing new world. With the facts before them, she realized it all meant little if action didn't follow, so she spearheaded an effort to get the world's political leaders together in one room to focus on solutions. The 1992 Earth Summit in Rio de Janeiro, Brazil, was born.

The Earth Summit focused on what Brundtland called "sustainable development," a term she coined to encompass environmental and human health, resource adequacy, and the growing divide on numerous issues between rich and poor nations. For many, it was a chance to tackle one specific problem that threatened to exacerbate all of the others—global climate change.

With a growing number of nations recognizing the potential benefits of dealing with climate change by applying the approach taken by the Montreal Protocol for dealing with ozone, the leaders at the summit signed the United Nations Framework Convention on Climate Change (UNFCCC). Short on specifics, the agreement provided for nations to gather annually and hammer out the details.

By 1997, the UNFCCC members set forth those details at their annual meeting in Kyoto, Japan. The resulting Kyoto

Protocol set measurable and binding targets for reducing all six greenhouse gases. It also called for the first internationally authorized use of a cap-and-trade system—like the one applied in the United States to SO_2—to accomplish those targets in the most cost-effective manner. Ironically, although Montreal was the political progenitor of Kyoto, it was also its nemesis. Trying to eliminate ozone-depleting emissions, Montreal committed nations to replace such chemicals with substitutes that were benign to atmospheric ozone, but which, it was later discovered, were hundreds of times more potent as heat-trapping, climate-changing pollutants.

Brundtland's third stint as prime minister had ended the year before the Kyoto meeting, but her fingerprints were clearly on the hoped-for result. As global environmental leaders, all standing on her formidable shoulders, boarded flights from Japan back to their home nations, she turned her attention to another global threat: smoking. By 2004, she was listed by London's *Financial Times* as the fourth most influential European of the last quarter century, just behind Pope John Paul II, Mikhail Gorbachev and Margaret Thatcher.

What Does the Kyoto Protocol Say?

In summary, here are the results produced by the Kyoto Protocol that are relevant to the Carbon Code:

- The European Union passed laws to reduce carbon below 1990 levels by 2012, and, for the most part, it has succeeded.
- The United States and Canada agreed to do likewise, and, although the United States never ratified the deal, about half the states and provinces have taken actions comparable to that commitment, as described in Appendix D, although they still won't get carbon emissions below 1990 levels much before 2020.
- China, India, and other developing nations agreed to reduce emissions by an unspecified amount, but their total emissions have since risen dramatically.

Although it may sound harsh to say so, the rest of the countries don't much matter in terms of significant contributions to the problem or the solution.

Out of this combined policy work, four major types of programs are expected to achieve most of the carbon reductions and create billions of dollars, yen, and euros in new sustainable jobs and businesses that are at the heart of the Carbon Code and are described in more detail elsewhere in this book:

- Energy efficiency programs (things such as insulating homes, replacing inefficient appliances and lighting, and installing better control systems)
- Renewable energy deployment (such as solar, wind, biomass, geothermal, and hydro)
- Clean car technology (hybrids, battery, hydrogen, and bio-fuels) and increased fuel-efficiency standards that also reduce tailpipe carbon emissions
- A cap-and-trade market for "carbon credits"

Going forward, the UN process and any successor agreements to the Kyoto Protocol will depend largely on the success of global carbon markets in the EU and United States so far. Appendix C describes those in more detail.

Sources

"Gro Harlem Brundtland," Wikipedia, http://en.wikipedia.org/wiki/Gro_Harlem_ Brundtland, accessed October 1, 2009.

Tamminen, Terry, Sasha Abelson, and Kristina Haddad. *Climate Change Handbook* (Santa Monica: Seventh Generation Advisors Press, 2009).

APPENDIX C

Global Cap-and-Trade Carbon Markets 101

The following is excerpted from the *Carbon Code Handbook*, the full content of which can be downloaded by visiting the www. TheCarbonCode.com.

How Cap-and-Trade Works

In order to effectively address climate change, several different mechanisms will be necessary to reduce emissions. One of the most widely recognized mechanisms is a cap-and-trade program.

Cap-and-trade is part of an emissions trading system created to reduce the amount of greenhouse gas (GHGs) emissions. The regulating entity determines a limit (or "cap") on the amount of GHG emissions that may be produced each year in a given region. The cap is gradually lowered, thereby requiring greater emissions reductions over time.

Each emitting installation is permitted to emit a specified number of tons of GHGs per year. In most cap-and-trade systems, a ton of carbon dioxide equivalent (CO_2e) is represented by one

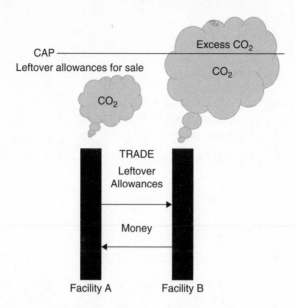

Figure C.1   How cap-and-trade works

allowance. The installation may be given these initial allowances (in a free-allocation system), purchase them in an auction, or obtain them in a combination of the two.

At the end of each year, regulated installations must hold enough allowances to cover the emissions created during that previous year. If an installation emits less than the allowed amount, its owners may sell or trade the surplus. If it emits more than the allowed amount, its owners must buy additional allowances from another party in order to comply with the cap.

Cap-and-trade works by establishing a price on carbon and by creating a supply and demand for it in a regulated market. When there is a shortage of allowances, the price will be driven up, thereby creating a financial incentive for firms to cut their emissions.

Compliance versus Voluntary Markets

A cap-and-trade program can exist in either a compliance or voluntary market. This is a key distinction that affects all aspects of cap-and-trade.

Compliance markets occur in countries where there is a regulated, mandatory cap-and-trade program. These countries set legally binding caps on GHG emissions. For example, Europe uses a mandatory cap-and-trade system called the European Union Emissions Trading System (EU ETS). This system was modeled in large part under the Kyoto Protocol (discussed in the Appendix A). The EU ETS has an emissions reductions commitment which is mandated and controlled by the government. Part of this system includes offset programs, which are regulated under the Clean Development Mechanism (CDM) and Joint Implementation (JI) program. The EU ETS is the largest emissions trading scheme within the global compliance market.

Voluntary markets operate in countries such as the United States that do not have a mandatory cap-and-trade program. These markets are often referred to as "unregulated" markets. In general, credits created in the voluntary market have less stringent control mechanisms and, as a result, are priced lower than credits in the compliance market.

There are no universally recognized credits within the voluntary markets. Credits are recognized only within the trading scheme that created them. In addition, there is no universal standard associated with the market, though many are emerging, such as the Voluntary Carbon Standard (VCS) and the Gold Standard (GS).

The United States has both voluntary and mandatory systems in place. The Chicago Climate Exchange is voluntary, however membership entails a legally binding commitment to reducing GHG emissions. The Regional Greenhouse Gas Initiative is a regional program that has implemented a mandatory cap on emissions for the electricity sector. The Western Climate Initiative is another regional program that is in the planning phase of creating an industry-wide cap-and-trade program for participating states.

Offsets

Offsets are another mechanism used to reduce GHG emissions and are often used in conjunction with a cap-and-trade program. An offset project is one that results in a measurable, verifiable reduction of GHG emissions. Offset credits are only issued if the offset project is able to demonstrate it resulted in greater emissions reductions than "business as usual" (BAU). Offset projects can be a cost-effective means to meet compliance obligations.

Types of offsets projects include:

- renewable energy (such as solar and wind);
- agriculture (such as methane sequestration and manure management);
- forestry (such as reforestation or REDD projects); and
- waste management (such as landfill methane capture and water management programs).

The Inner Workings of Carbon Markets

With the previous overview in mind, it may be useful to understand the mechanics and timing of the major regional cap-and-trade systems in more detail and how each one deals with carbon credits generated by offset programs.

The European Union Emissions Trading System (EU ETS)

The EU ETS is the largest multicountry, mandatory GHG cap-and-trade scheme worldwide. It is the world's largest emissions trading system and forms the cornerstone of the EU's strategy for meeting its emission-reduction targets cost-effectively.

Under the Kyoto Protocol, the European Union agreed to reduce its GHG emissions by 8 percent below 1990 levels by 2012. This target was modified to allow countries that have a greater ability to cut emissions (such as Germany, Denmark, and the U.K.) to take on tougher targets, while other countries are allowed to let their emissions grow (providing that the overall regional goal is met). For compliance purposes the group of countries within the EU ETS is essentially treated as a single entity.

The EU ETS covers approximately 12,000 installations across the 27 Member States of the European Union plus Iceland, Liechtenstein, and Norway. Each member is required to draft a

National Allocation Plan (NAP), which then must be approved by the European Commission. The NAP sets out how the annual allotment of carbon credits will be divided between the GHG emitters and sets limits for each individual emitter (or installation).

In order to make sure that real trading emerges and that emissions are reduced, EU governments must ensure that the total amount of allowances issued to installations is less than the amount that would have been emitted under a business–as–usual scenario. Every year, each installation is required to report actual GHG emissions. If the installation emits less than it was permitted to do, it will have a surplus of allowances which may then be sold. Conversely, if the installation emits more than permitted, it has two options: (1) purchase additional credits from an installation with a surplus in order to comply with the mandatory cap; and (2) offset its excess emissions through a CDM project or JI project (as discussed above).

Offsets in the EU ETS

The Kyoto Protocol sanctioned the use of carbon offsets as another way for governments and private companies to earn tradable credits through the creation of an offset project. Offset projects often occur in locations (mostly in developing countries) where the cost of the project is lower than it would be in the originating country, but result in emissions reductions that have global benefits. Offsets offer a flexible and cost-efficient means for a regulated party to fulfill their Kyoto Protocol or EU ETS commitments, while the developing country receives investments in clean technology.

Currently there are two major types of offset projects that are permitted under the Kyoto Protocol's emissions trading scheme, Joint Implementation (JI), and Clean Development Mechanism (CDM).

JI projects occur in industrialized countries or in a country with an "economy in transition" (many JI projects occur in Eastern European countries, the greatest number in the Czech Republic, Poland, and Hungary). JI serves as a valuable alternative to domestic emissions reductions. In order to be eligible for a JI project, the country must be a member of the Kyoto Protocol and must meet requirements set out by the UNFCCC.

CDM projects occur in developing countries, the majority in China, India, Mexico, and Brazil. The industrialized country that creates the project must obtain the consent of the developing host country. In addition, all methods used must be approved by the CDM Executive Board (EB).

Regional Greenhouse Gas Initiative (RGGI)

The Regional GHG Initiative (RGGI) is a cooperative effort by ten Northeast and Mid-Atlantic states and is the first mandatory, market-based effort in the United States to reduce greenhouse gas emissions. The program initially covers only CO_2 emissions from power plants in the region. RGGI may be extended to include additional sources of carbon emissions as well as GHGs other than CO_2. By 2018, RGGI intends to reduce CO_2 emissions from the power sector 10 percent from its baseline (which is taken from the average annual emissions of each installation from 2002–2004).

The member states of RGGI are Connecticut, Delaware, Maine, Maryland, Massachusetts, New Hampshire, New Jersey, New York, Rhode Island, and Vermont (see Figure C.2). CO_2 allowances issued by any participating state are usable across all state programs. Therefore, the ten individual states, in aggregate, form one regional compliance market for CO_2 emissions.

The majority of CO_2 allowances issued by each participating state are distributed through quarterly auctions. The proceeds of the auction are invested in energy efficiency, renewable energy, and other clean energy projects. RGGI hopes to spur innovation in the clean energy economy and create green jobs in each state.

The Western Climate Initiative (WCI)

The Western Climate Initiative (WCI) was launched in February 2007, initially as a collaboration by the governors of Arizona,

California, New Mexico, Oregon, and Washington to develop regional strategies to address climate change. WCI is evaluating and implementing ways to reduce GHGs within the member states and have set an overall goal for reducing GHG emissions in the region. The partners developed a plan to guide this work and actively seek public input throughout the process. Since its inception, WCI has grown to include several more states of the United States and Mexico and provinces of Canada, some as full members and others as observers (see Figure C.2).

The WCI program is expected to launch in 2012. When WCI is fully implemented in 2015, it expects to cover nearly 90 percent of the GHG emissions in WCI member states and provinces. WCI is also working on complementary policies that support the cap-and-trade portion of the program, which will provide additional opportunities to address climate change and achieve related benefits such as increased energy efficiency, increased renewable energy generation, improved air quality and reduced water pollution, job growth, and increased provincial, state, and local revenue.

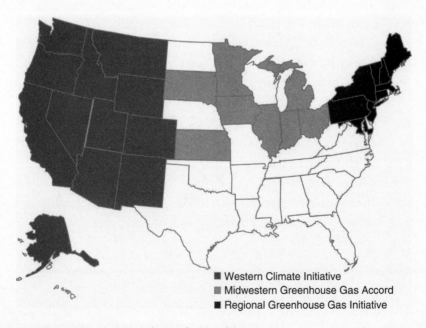

■ Western Climate Initiative
■ Midwestern Greenhouse Gas Accord
■ Regional Greenhouse Gas Initiative

Figure C.2   Cap-and-trade markets in the United States

Midwestern Greenhouse Gas Reduction Accord (MGGRA)

The MGGRA is a regional agreement by Midwestern states and a Canadian province to reduce GHG emissions and combat climate change (see Figure C.2). The accord is the first cap-and-trade program to be designed for the midwestern region.

The Midwestern GHG Reduction Accord Advisory Group has finalized their recommendations and the members are now reviewing them to move on to the next steps to be taken in the region and at the federal level. The recommendations are from the advisory group only, and have not been endorsed or approved by individual governors (or Canadian premiers).

Source

Tamminen, Terry, Sasha Abelson, and Kristina Haddad. *Climate Change Handbook* (Santa Monica: Seventh Generation Advisors Press, 2009).

States Taking Action on Carbon

In the absence of federal carbon legislation in the United States, many states have created their own laws, policies, and low-carbon incentive programs to address the growing concerns about climate change. These efforts are primarily organized around four basic components:

1. State laws, such as California's Global Warming Solutions Act of 2006 (AB32), which set limits on carbon emissions and mandate reductions over time.
2. Climate action plans, which set targets for carbon reductions (some of which are derived from state laws) like member nations in the UNFCCC and Kyoto Protocol. These plans articulate policies that will achieve the target reductions.
3. Renewable portfolio standards (RPSs) establish requirements that utilities obtain a specified percentage of energy from low-carbon, renewable sources by certain dates. This is a major component of most state climate action plans, but also exists in states without such comprehensive plans;

4. Participation in a cap-and-trade system, such as RGGI, WCI, and MWGGRA (see Appendix C).

States have also adopted building and appliance energy-efficiency standards and policies, such as California's vehicle emissions standard, as key elements of their climate action plans. Many of these programs have since been adopted by the federal government and thus created national standards.

The maps in Figures D.1 through D.3 depict the key policies being undertaken at the state level.

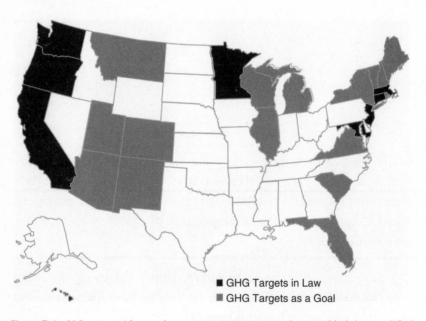

Figure D.1   U.S. states with greenhouse gas emissions targets. States in black have codified one or more targets in state law; states in gray have declared targets via executive order or other means

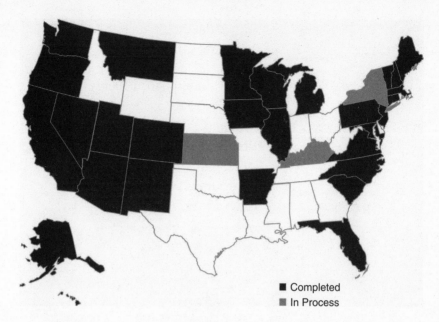

Figure D.2   U.S. states with climate action plans (or equivalent policies). States in black have completed climate action plans; states in gray have plans in process

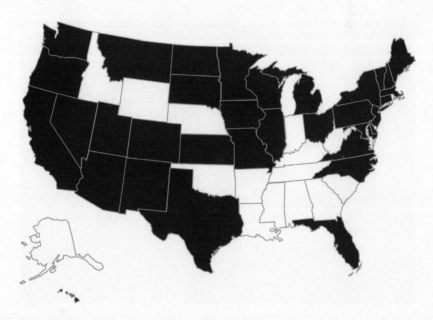

Figure D.3   U.S. states with renewable portfolio standards

INDEX